Shattered Dreams

A Novel By

Mike Curry

Front Cover Image by Peter "Digital Dream" & Unseen Handz Media
Book Design by Unseen Handz Media
Editor: Unseen Handz Administration
First printing edition 2020 in the United States

Unseen Handz Media, LLC
1206 Motor Avenue
Helena, MT 59602

Acknowledgement

I would like to say thanks to my Unseen Handz Media team, also to all those who supported and waited for the release of this book. I promise you won't be disappointed. Writing has been my passion for so many years and it's a blessing for me to come out with such quality material that's pertinent to what I and others have experienced in this lifetime.

I would like to give a shout out to my marketing team which is spearheaded by my mother Sharon, thanks for the support and guidance you have given me since the day I was born, you knew I had a talent of-and skill that the world never knew existed. The blessing of my life Patrice and Ma Sugar and the whole Alves family. To Ron Pelton the man who walked me through each chapter at the early stages of this book. I appreciate you Ron and if you read this just know this book could and would have never been done without you. To all my Curry, Simpson and Polite family thanks for the support. My brothers Bay and Rell thanks for supporting me. My Grove Hall neighborhood thanks for the support I appreciate it thoroughly and to my dawg BOX who helped me shape and mold the main character in this book. I love you bro. I would also like to say thanks to those who loved the first book **"3 Pounds of Pressure"**. Last but not least thanks to all those who believed in me and wanted to see me do better and think better. I appreciate all the support it means a lot to me.

Thanks
Mike Curry

Words from the Author

In life many people possess a skill-set that stands out above the rest and it's often that their dreams get shattered by many different reasons that can hamper one's ability to think rationally. It takes a strong-willed person to overcome such and become greater than he/she was before their dream was shattered.

This book Shattered Dreams is part of the 3 Pounds of Pressure series and this story depicts the life of a teenager growing up in one of the worst housing projects in the entire New England. Growing up in Boston was a challenge for many including myself, but it took pitfall after pitfall to realize what my true dream was. My focus on this book is to capture the reader's attention and bring awareness to how rampant crime occurs and becomes repetitive in a family's history.

During the late 1980s and the early 1990s Boston, like many other major cities, experienced a sudden increase in youth homicides. Between 1990 and 1994 the amount of youth homicides in those years had never been duplicated and earned the city of Boston the name "The Bloody Bean" and the "Los Angeles of the East Coast."

"The black kids who inspire the fear seem not merely Un-recognizable but alien," calling young people who came into contact with the justice system "radically impulsive, brutally remorseless"

-John Dilulio
1996

The youth violence in the city at that time was similar to other major cities, but what separated Boston from other major cities was not only the high level of youth violence, but the street gangs who claimed turf such as housing projects and side streets as their own. They found a unique way to separate themselves from others by claiming allegiance to sport franchises memorabilia by way of adopting sport teams as their own. Over time any sport franchise one can name was associated with a street or housing project in Boston with some gangs even claiming allegiance to the same sport franchise.

One of the major problems that revolve crime in inner-cities across America are the age of the participants who participate in the crimes that occur in their communities and abroad.

As crime in the inner-city continues to spiral out of control the public fear continues to be fueled by media coverage and by "tough-on-crime" stances taken by many public officials. In the late eighties and the early nineties most of the crime committed were by juveniles who were entering the thug lifestyle. The main component that is often ignored and needs to be addressed is the social conditions (urban school system, poverty-stricken communities, and single parents) that these youths reside in. Many of them undervalue their lives because they don't understand the importance of their worth so the solution became how they were raised in the playpen which ultimately lead to the state or federal pen.

In this book as well as my other book **"3 Pounds of Pressure"** my intention was not to glorify the street culture of Boston, but try to get the readers to understand of the origin of how fragile an adolescent mind may be when growing up in inner-city areas where role models are those with whom they see daily. I took a different approach by expounding on how laws are created, growing up in a single-family household and how dreams can easily be shattered in the community you proclaim to love. I had dreams myself that was shattered by incarceration and I overcame them fears of being a failure by finding out my true skills and talent and making something out of them. I advise those who once had a dream that was shattered to use that experience and make your life better and you will reap the rewards of your rebound.

Thank you for taking your time out to read Shattered Dreams, I hope you enjoyed it.

Prologue

Daniel Levi was a Jewish middle aged, tall, slim state representative whose family name held weight on Beacon Hill. His family was responsible for several bills that were created into law. He sat in the rear seat of his Gold Mercedes as he was being driven to his home in Newton, Massachusetts by his chauffeur.

Every day after work he drove through different neighborhoods in Boston so that he could see how much the city changed since he was a child.

"My family was significant in helping train the country's Hebrew teachers and set Jewish education standards." Levi thought as he saw hoodlum after hoodlum posted on corners of Blue Hill Avenue. He still remembered all the stories that his family had told him about the Jews that inhabited Blue Hill Avenue back when it was nicknamed Jew Hill Avenue. *"We left because of the racial tensions of the Irish-Americans and the migration of the African-Americans from the south. It was not safe to walk the streets anymore,"* he remembers his father saying to him. *"Even the banks were against us, they were mad because they could not collect interest or profit from the mortgages that we already paid off. We were induced to sell our properties cheap and block by block, the authorities converted the buildings we had owned into low-income housing, offering reduced mortgages to the influx of African-American families."*

"There are so many young hoodlums walking the streets committing violent crimes. Something has to be done to stop these animals from tearing up the streets that my family has helped build. Levi thought as his driver drove down Columbus Ave. "Turn onto Centre Street." He ordered.

As the driver drove past Jackson Square Levi saw a couple young hoodlums selling drugs outside of the Bromley-Heath Street Project. *"This is the worst housing project in New England."* He thought, as he stared at what he would know as the slums.

"It all starts with an idea." He said, as he started to formulate mentally what he felt can be a solution to the crime problem in the city of Boston. *"Boston has a reputation to uphold and if these animals keep giving others reasons to slander the name of the city then they will be where they deserve to be. They are the reasons why my family had to take flight out in the suburbs and in time we will reclaim our city back one way or another."*

The solution that Levi had in mind was creating a law aimed at tackling the juvenile crime problem. His ideology was if he could get the minority youth entrapped in the system, then about time they reach adulthood they would still experience the same criminal behavior that would eventually lead them to lengthy federal prison sentences. He understood the psychology of the mind and decided to flip what he knew and aim it at those he felt would hinder him, his family and other Jews to reclaim back, the city that they had helped made prominent.

Chapter 1

The Bromley-Heath street project was located on 25 acres of land in the Jamaica Plain section of Boston. The housing project was originally three adjoining low rent developments; Heath Street, which was built in 1941, Bromley Park, which was built in 1952 and Bickford Street, which was built in 1964. The three developments offer 840 units making it the largest housing project in the entire New England. In the late eighties new entrance steps, canopies, windows and roofs at Bromley Park were designed providing more color and decoration at the entrances. The residents of the housing project call the Bromley Park area of the project the New Side. While the Heath Street side of the project was dubbed the Old Side.

Bromley-Heath Street was the first housing project in the United States to be run by tenants instead of a government agency. The tenants in the project were mostly linked to three families: The Johnsons, the Taylors and the Bartons. There were smaller families but none bigger than these three. One family stood out and that family was the Barton's.

Mrs. Mary Barton and Susan Johnson were the founders of the Bromley-Heath Tenant Management Corp. The Barton's ran the project internally and externally and the matriarch was Mrs. Mary Barton, the executive director of the tenant management Association. She was able to score several rent-free apartments on the new side of the project. Her apartment, that the residents called the Palatial, was a single bedroom, wall to wall carpeted unit that had giant screen televisions plastered all over the apartment.

Mrs. Mary Barton had 13 children. Her children spawned 41 grandchildren and 7 great grandchildren, making the Barton's the largest and most influential family in project history. Her third oldest child Raymond "Greenback" Barton was the drug lord who supplied the project. He distributed large and small amounts of heroin and cocaine throughout the project. No one couldn't do anything in the project without him getting a percentage. He was very protective of his siblings especially his younger sister Lynn.

Evelyn "Lynn" Barton became pregnant at the tender age of fifteen by an infamous stick up kid named Alf Taylor. Alf was part of the notorious Taylor Clan, which was just as large as the Barton clan, but with less influence in the project. The Taylor's resided on the Bromley Park side while the Barton's resided on the Bickford side.

Alf made his moves in the project as head of a notorious stick-up team called the "Heat makers". The day Lynn went into labor, he and his team were out on a big caper. One thing led to another and a shooting ensued, resulting in his being arrested on the happiest day of his baby mother's life and the worst day of his, as he tried, convicted and sentenced to serve 35-40 years in the state prison in Walpole, Massachusetts.

Lynn named her son after him, but she gave her child the Barton last name. With Big Alf upstate and being a single mother at sixteen, Lynn was doomed and turned to her mother for support. Her mother gave her a rent-free apartment at 138 Heath Street. Her brother, Greenback supplied her with the new furniture and gave her a weekly allowance to help her and her newborn son.

The yearn for a man in her life made Lynn a hot target for all the hustlers outside the project as she made her way to nightclubs like Estelle's, Fundo's, 3C's, Kay's Oasis, the Roxy and others around the city. She played the flirt game heavy as she enticed each hustler with small conversation, but deep down she knew she couldn't bring any of them back to the project: her gung-ho twin brothers Terrence and Clarence weren't hearing it, for they were heavily protective of their little sister.

Around the time her son Alfred was reaching eleven years old, she met a hustler from the Mattapan area of the city nicknamed Mr. Millionaire for his flamboyant ways. There wasn't a hustler in the city that was more flamboyant and dramatic than him. In the winter time he donned full length mink, sable and chinchilla fur coats and in the summer, he was decked in gaudy jewelry, silks and gator shoes. He was "the man" and his drug of choice was the heroin that he distributed all over the city. He was loved by all and hated by none. He was more of Lynn's likeness, for he had light brown eyes, pretty features and strapped for cash. She saw Dollar signs the day he pulled up in a black seven series BMW with gold trimming and piping. She was in awe of his A.C. Schnitzler kit and how deep-dished his gold Dayton's were. What she didn't know was that her son was jealous of their relationship and he hated that his mother was falling in love with another man who wasn't his father and he also felt that the time she had spent with him was taking away from the time they used to spend together.

A year into the relationship everything was going good for all, her brothers agreed to the relationship. Including Greenback. He started using his sister as bait to get his heroin cheaper. The day Lynn's son Alfred turned twelve years old, Mr. Millionaire funded an all-expense paid shopping spree for him at the local malls. He copped Alfred a solid gold dookie rope that cost ten thousand. What Alfred saw was what he thought was an engagement ring flooded with colorful diamonds that Mr. Millionaire brought from the store Tiffany's.

"My mother isn't going to marry no one but my father," Alfred thought to himself.

Mr. Millionaire liked the quiet boy, but what he didn't know was that it was vice versa in Alfred's mind. Alfred played the part like he was content, for he was only waiting for an opportunity to strike and do his father a favor.

Chapter 2

Alfred stayed outside while his mother and her boyfriend went upstairs. He sat on the project bench on his 12th birthday showing his little crew, who called themselves the baby Heath Mob, all the jewelry that Mr. Millionaire brought him. Alfred made it seem in their eyes everything was good but in his mind it truly wasn't. He was a selfish nigga and felt like Mr. Millionaire preyed on his mother's weakness for gifts, affection and love. Alfred was not letting anyone's riches buy out his mother's love. He first looked at his twin uncles Clarence and Terrence in front of a project building as they hustled and then over at his older cousins Crime and O-Dawg who stood on some project stairs shooting dice. He knew that the Taylor and the Barton clan would have his back, whether he was right or wrong and that he was going to use it to his advantage. He dapped up his crew and walked toward his building and up the stairs and stuck his key in the door. The screams from his mother's bedroom told him that Mr. Millionaire's dick was eating her guts alive as they were into heavy sex. The screams infuriated him as he tiptoed to the kitchen, and grabbed a steak knife, walked to his room, sat down and watched television. He saw Mr. Millionaire's clothes scattered around the house. He dozed off for a few hours and woke up in the wee hours of the morning.

"Oh! Shit!" He said, as he got up and kicked off his Adidas Torsions sneakers that Mr. Millionaire had brought him for his birthday, grabbed the steak knife and crept toward his mother's bedroom. He placed his ear to the door and listened. He heard music, turned the door knob and was surprised that it was open. He walked in on his tippy toes, crept around the side of the bed where Mr. Millionaire laid. and placed the knife to his neck and in one sweet stroke sliced it from ear to ear. He jumped back as blood squirted out into the air, onto the ceiling and all over the bed. He backed up and smiled, having just committed his first murder for the love of his father. He left the room the same way he came in: on his tippy toes. He left the door slightly open, stepped back into the roof and stashed it. He looked down into the projects and spotted his cousins Crime and O-Dawg and went to join them out front, as they hustled drugs on the graveyard shift.

"Young boy! What are you doing out here?" Crime asked, surprised to see Alfred outside.

"Today's my birthday and it's a big, big day for me."

"Big day huh! What are you little nigga like thirteen or fourteen?" His other cousin O-Dawg asked.

"Nah! Twelve."

"Damn! Your little ass moves like you're older," O-Dawg said, as he heard a loud scream.

"Yo! You heard that?" Crime said as he looked to see where the scream came from.

"That's my mother. She must have woken up and saw the damage." Alfred said as he opened the project door.

"Come on, let me show you what I'm about these days." Alfred said as he led his cousins upstairs to the apartment. He opened the door and saw that his mother's negligee was drenched in blood.

"What happened?" Her nephew Crime asked, as he came to her aid.

"I don't know. Come here and look." She said as she led them into her bedroom.

"I woke up and he was choking on his own blood." She said.

Both brothers looked at each other and remembered what their little cousin told them. They shook their head and wondered why. Lynn looked at her son and then at her nephew. What she heard crushed her.

"I know what happened, for I killed the bastard. I did my father, me and you a favor." He said as he leaned on the wall with no care in the world.

"At his funeral, tell him 'thank you' for the Adidas Torsions. I'm going to wear them in his memory."

"Damn little nigga, you got your Bones now," Crime said to his little cousin.

From that day on the name "Bones" stuck with him. The next-door neighbor heard Lynn scream and called 911.

A knock on the door made them all jump back, then, Lynn marched to the door and looked through the peephole. Her eyes got wide as she saw two uniformed police officers. Damn, the police." She said, as she hurried back to the room. She kneeled down and grabbed her son by the hand and cried as she spoke her next words. "You're going to have to tell the police you killed him, there's nothing they can do to you because you are under the age of thirteen" She said.

"Oh shit! I have some crack on me," Crime said as he opened the window for him and his brother to climb out.

Lynn watched as they climbed out of the window and turned toward her son and said. "You have to man up and take responsibility for your actions."

Alfred just looked at his mother as he nodded his head up and down, agreeing._The uniformed police officers came into the apartment and asked Lynn, "Is there a problem?

Lynn shook her head speechless, and pointed to her bedroom. The police officers walked into her room and were stopped dead in their tracks as they saw all the blood on the floor, bed and ceiling. They walked to the body and saw Mr. Millionaire's open eyes staring at the ceiling.

Lynn grabbed her son and held him in her arms. She watched as they radioed in for an ambulance, the coroner and the homicide division. A few more cruisers pulled up and cordoned off the front of the project building with yellow caution tape, next came the ambulance and the Lieutenant of the homicide division, a redneck named Anthony "Mr. Homicide" Sterner. He earned the name Mr. Homicide by the many people he was accused of gunning down in the line of duty. He was investigated by the department several times only to end up with the same result: Justified. He walked inside the apartment wearing his blue windbreaker with the word Homicide in yellow lettering scrawled across the back.

Mr. Homicide had a yellow pad in his left hand, a pen in his ear and a camera in his right hand. He passed the pad to one of the detectives and walked into the room.

"Ms. Barton, long time no see. What's it been seven year since your brother's death? Is your family still putting in those frivolous lawsuits against the department?"

Lynn just looked at him like he was crazy, then turned her head sideways, puckered up her lips and spit in his face.

"ARREST HER FOR ASSAULT ON A POLICE OFFICER," He yelled to a uniformed police officer, as saliva dripped down his face.

"Take me with her, because I'm the murderer," Alfred said.

"What!" This admission caught him off guard.

"You heard him," Lynn said, as she was getting handcuffed.

Mr. Homicide looked at Bones and asked him, "What's your name?"

"Bones." Alfred blurted out with his high-pitched voice.

"How old are you?"

"Twelve."

"Damn, too young," he mumbled a little too loud.

"They need to change the laws to get rug rats like this off the streets. Take them both to the headquarters." Mr. Homicide ordered the officers.

"OH, SHIT! SOMEBODY GOT KILLED, THERE GOES THE CORONERS TRUCK," a female voice yelled out.

Greenback watched the uniformed police officers march his little sister and his nephew out of the building into a cruiser.

"Sterner, the bedroom window was open. I think we have an accessory after the fact," his partner Wrinkle Head, said.

"Let the investigation begin. I need to know all the facts of what happened and why that window was left open. I know the guy in there. They call him Mr. Millionaire, for all the millions he had around the city. He's from a large family in the Mattapan area of the city," Mr. Homicide said as he walked out of the apartment and down the stairs.

Greenback watched as Mr. Homicide came out of the building. He stared at him until they caught eye contact, then raised his finger and made it into a gun and pulled the trigger.

Chapter 3

The Boston Herald van pulled up and parked on the sidewalk. The journalist hopped out and spoke to one of the detectives while holding a white notepad in her hand.

Greenback picked up his phone and dialed his lawyer's house number. He knew this case was going to be a high-profile case and he thought about the headlines in the next day's Boston Herald: "*Twelve-year-old killed his mother's boyfriend in the notorious Bromley-Heath Street housing project.*"

Lynn and her son were escorted down to the police headquarters. Lynn was placed in a room and handcuffed to the leg of a long rectangular table. The room was bland, with the exception of a projection screen, coat rack and a coffee maker. "*This must be a meeting room,*" she thought. She knew that the charge she was being arrested for was minimal compared to what her son was facing, but "*what could they do to an twelve-year-old?*" she thought, already knowing the answer to her question. The laws in Massachusetts were lenient for a juvenile and she knew that they weren't going to get information from her: she would let her son do all the talking.

Twenty minutes later a few detectives came in with Mr. Homicide. One of the detectives had a tape recorder, the other had a notepad and a pen in each hand. She watched Mr. Homicide closely as he took off his windbreaker, hung it on the coat rack, stretched his arms in an intimidating manner then walked over to the table and placed his hands on it and snarled.

"Hello! Evelyn. Are you done spitting or you need a muzzle for that mouth of yours? I'm going to ask you a few questions and you are going to answer them and if not then I'm going to make sure you get an accessory after the fact." He laughed, as he turned on the tape recorder and asked her his first question.

"Where were you when the stabbing happened?"

"In my bed sleep," Lynn said with her pretty girl smirk.

"In the bed, huh?"

"Yeah! In my bed sleep."

"What happened?"

"I don't know, didn't I tell you I was in my bed sleeping," Lynn said, now with an attitude. She was still in a state of shock of what her son had done.

"I believe you; I believe you not one bit. How could an Eleven-year-old come in and stab his mother's boyfriend and she stays asleep?"

"Nah! That's where you went wrong, I didn't say, 'I was still asleep when it happened you asked me' where was I when it happened."

"Well, what did you see after the fact?"

"I plead the fifth. I need my attorney," she said as she watched one of the detectives stop writing and the other turn off the tape recorder.

"You could have your lawyer but it isn't going to save your son. He already admitted to the crime," he said as he tried to bluff her into admitting her involvement in the crime. He knew the state couldn't do anything because of his age.

* * * * * *

Greenback called an emergency meeting in the Bromley Hall with his family. He watched, as one family member after another marched into the hall tired, confused, depressed and stressed. He walked up to his mother, hugged her and whispered in her ear. "Everything is going to be alright."

"What happened?" Mrs. Mary Barton asked.

"I don't know, I know that Alfred murdered his mother's boyfriend."

"Oh, My lord!" She said as her hand covered her mouth.

"Don't worry mom, I already got two of the best paid attorneys on it as we speak."

"I hope so, because the B.H.A. (Boston Housing Authority) is going to investigate the situation and the T.M.C." Mrs. Mary said with a worried look on her face, "I have to do something to give the project a better image," she said and shaking her head at the bad news.

Greenback, was the only one who spoke. He told his family to appear at Roxbury courthouse, Monday to support their sister, aunt, nephew and cousin. After the meeting with the family he walked around the project rounding up all the hustlers and arranged a meeting in the community center known as the Cave.

One by one they all came to the Cave. Once the whole room was filled with the Bromley-Heath Mob he began his lecture about the necessity of his crew showing up at Roxbury Courthouse to support his family.

The Heath-Mob adopted the colors of red and black and were known to dress in the Miami Heat memorabilia. They all nodded their heads in agreement to every word the project kingpin spoke. Greenback knew he was the undisputed king of the project and used the power he had to his advantage. He remembered when he was known in the project as a good kid who had basketball skills.

"I came a long way," he thought, "penalties would be handed out to anyone who doesn't show up to court on Monday."

He looked at his Rolex watch, and then at the table Heath-Mob and smiled, "I see y'all Monday at the courthouse."

Chapter 4

Lynn was escorted from the headquarters to the police station, where she was booked for assault on a police officer. She was fingerprinted, booked and posed for a mugshot. Her mugshot was on pretty girl status as she smiled showing her dimples. She knew if the picture was to show up in the paper, she wanted it to be on pretty girl status.

Alfred was in a darkened dungeon-like cell that held juveniles. He was in the cell, lying on the wooden butcher block, thinking about his new name "Bones". He liked it a lot. He knew the name would stick long as he enforced it. He thought long and hard about what his mother told him and knew she would never lie to him. He smiled as he remembered clearly her words verbatim: ``they can't do anything to you because you are under Thirteen years old.''

Bones had faith in his mother and his massive family. He knew that, once his uncle Greenback got wind of the situation, he would make sure they get the best defense. After they finished booking his mother, they took him out of the cell and escorted him to the booking area. He looked in the hallway and saw the homicide detective filling out paperwork. He looked at him long and hard until he looked up at him and shook his head and said "I'm going to make you remember me."

Mr. Homicide laughed and continued doing what he was doing and without looking he stated lowly: "Your family already know what I have done."

Bones was confused by the statement, turned toward the booking officer and started the process by giving his personal information. Then, he went on to do his fingerprints and mugshot. His lazy eye showed in the picture.

Bones knew he had created a new enemy with the homicide detective and didn't give a fuck. He wanted the streets to know his name and, if this murder wasn't the reason, then he was going to strike again.

Two hours later Bones was awoken, handcuffed and shackled, and escorted to juvenile hall to start the process. The officer who escorted him took the chains that held his wrist and ankles, turned over the paperwork and then left.

"Barton," the burly white staff yelled out.

"Right here!" Bones said raising his hand.

"You're here with us for the weekend. We're going to ask you a few questions, strip you, and place you in the shower to clean yourself. Here, take this," he said, as he tossed Bones a blue jumpsuit. "Then once we are finished, we are going to feed you and assign you to a bed."

"That's what's up," Bones said as he looked at how clean the place was.

Bones followed the procedure and went into the room with his bag lunch.

The room had ten beds in a row. He wondered who was there as he looked at four lumps under the blankets. He looked out at the oversized window and knew this was the beginning of his criminal history. He ate the bag lunch and saved the apple and laid in his bed with his arms behind his head. He closed his eyes and dozed off in a deep sleep.

* * * * * *

While Bones was asleep at juvenile hall his grandmother, Mrs. Mary Barton held an emergency meeting with the Tenant Management Corp in her office. She knew that something had to be done to erase the bad publicity that was sure to come. She wanted to create a resident security force and implement new strategies in the project.

"We need a security force patrolling the project." Mrs. Mary started off the meeting.

"I could talk to Straughter Security or even the Wackenhut security and see if we could hire them. Mary, you know the Boston Housing Authority won't fund the idea. We are the overseers of this housing development," Mrs. Susan Johnson said.

"Your right, but I was thinking about creating a resident security force, which our trucks that have Bromley-Heath security painted on their side doors," Mrs. Mary replied.

"That's a good idea," Mrs. Johnson said, as she applauded her partner for quick thinking.

"What about a new health care facility?" One of the other activists asked.

"We have the Martha Elliot Health Center. We could create an adjoining drug treatment and education center to help all the addicts in the project. It's the kids, the future generation, that need to be saved," she said, as her thoughts revolved about the atrocious act her grandson Alfred had committed.

"Good idea, for it would be the first of its kind in the city," Mrs. Johnson agreed.

Chapter 5

Monday morning the media were in full effect, tripods, news trucks, reporters and correspondents posted outside of the courthouse.

The Barton's came out in full force they came to support Bones and Lynn thirty-two deep. They walked through the courthouse metal detectors and up toward the second floor. Bones father family, the Taylors, were already in the courthouse waiting for Bones' name to be called.

Greenback was the last of the Barton's to arrive. He pulled up with the two super lawyers, he had paid to represent his little sister and nephew. He saluted all the men in his family with hugs and handshakes and all the females with kisses on the cheeks, lips and hands. He walked over to his mother, held her hand and kissed it.

"Good morning, Raymond! We are going to implement a security force in the project," His mother said.

"Security!" Greenback said shocked at what his mother had told him.

"Yes! We are going to name it Bromley-Heath Security."

Thoughts flooded his mind as he thought about an interference with his empire. He had his mind made up and knew if the security got in his way of becoming the next millionaire in the city, shots would be fired. He looked at his mother and smiled. He knew her choice was because of the bad publicity the family was getting for his nephew actions.

"Have you read the papers?" Mrs. Mary asked, as she looked her son in the eyes.

"Yes! I read the articles."

"Bad publicity isn't good for the family name, Raymond."

Greenback knew his mother was telling the truth and with the murder in his family name, the heat would be on. He knew in order to stay on top of the drug game, he had to stay under the radar. A black sheriff van rolled into the parking lot. He turned around and looked.

"Damn, look at all those Miami Heat hats," a juvenile said, as he looked out the window of the van at the members of the Heath-Mob "They must be from Heath Street."

Bones looked out the back of the van. The first person he saw was his father's brother Larry Taylor. "Damn, even uncle Larry came to represent."

The van took a turn and stopped at the back entrance of the courthouse. Minutes later the latches on the door were snapped. The bright sunlight blasted through the van as the door opened. Four court officers were standing there with a list of names.

"BARTON." The officer yelled.

Bones stepped forward out of the van and was ushered upstairs. He was placed in a cell with a few juveniles who came from various detention centers around the city. Bones was the youngest in the cell and perhaps in the system. He walked around the cell with a mad dog stare.

"Marv! Look at the little nigga's ice grill," hollered a tough juvenile named "Horror" from Ruggles project.

"I see him," Marv said, as he laughed at the mad dog stare on Bones' face.

A member of the Orchard Park Trailblazer Gang who went by the name of Monster walked in the cell. Bones stared at the behemoth juvenile and wondered where he was from.

"OPTB," Monster shouted, as he walked around the cell with a smile on his face.

"Oh, that nigga's from O.P." Bones said to himself, as he walked over toward Monster and reached out his hand for a shake. "I'm from the P!" Bones said.

"You know the Heat and O.P. is fam. My name is Monster. What do they call you?"

"Bones."

While Bones and Monster were getting to know each other, Crime looked at his younger brother, "what you want to do in retaliation for our father?"

"You already know," O-Dawg said as his heart raced in anticipation.

"Come on!" Evelyn's case is being heard," her lawyer said, as he came over to where Greenback and his mother stood.

Crime and O-dawg followed their uncle's lead as he walked into the courtroom.

Lynn sat behind a partition glass with a few other females. She smiled as her family marched in the courtroom. She knew her family was going to be there in full force. She watched her brother Greenback sit in the back of the courtroom and nod to her. She nodded back and then looked at her lawyer and thanked GOD that her older brother had money.

The judge presiding over the case was the most liberal judge in the courthouse. With his soft heart, Lynn's lawyer believed that she would be able to get Lynn released on personal recognizance or a low bail. Either way, she was going home today.

The judge listened to the district attorney and then her well-spoken lawyer. It was her lawyer who had persuaded his judgement. He set another date and released Lynn on personal recognizance.

As the court officers un-cuffed Lynn, she looked at Mr. Homicide and flashed the same pretty girl smile that she gave for her mugshot.

* * * * * *

Bones was in the cell talking to Monster about the streets when a court officer appeared at the cell.

"BARTON, come on buddy, it's your turn to see the judge."

Bones gave Monster the Orchard Park and Heath Street double dap handshake and walked toward the door. The court officer opened the door, placed the cuffs on his wrist and escorted him down the stairs into a hallway, where a few adults were posted waiting their turn to see

Judge Black.

"That's a little kid," a female voice exclaimed.

"What has he done?" Another added.

The court officer opened the door and Bones stepped inside the courtroom. He looked at his father's side of the family. He looked deeper and saw a few faces who were unrecognizable. The sound of a child call for his mother got his attention. As he looked for the source, he saw a pretty light skin female grab the child arm and leave the courtroom.

The door swung closed. It opened seconds later and the Matriarch, Mrs. Mary Barton stepped in followed by a long line of family members. The last one to come in was his mother. She smiled at Bones and touched her heart.

Judge Black came out of his chambers and looked at the packed courtroom. He looked at Bones and then down at the docket sheet.

Bones knew he had nothing coming by how harsh the judge had been toward his lawyer. He listened closely as his lawyer argued about the juvenile laws for those older than thirteen years of age.

"You're right Mrs. Curran. The law doesn't apply to Alfred Barton, but what I'm going to do is make him a ward of the state and send him to a mental health treatment center to be evaluated. Court is adjourned," the judge said, as he banged his gavel.

Bones looked at his family with a confused look. He knew nothing would stop him from being around his mother, not even the treatment center.

Lynn was pissed that the judge had handed her son over to the Department of Children and Families. She felt a few tears trickle down her cheek.

"Wipe those tears away, big girls don't cry," Greenback said, as he hugged his sister.

Lynn wiped the tears away and looked over at her mother, who was inundated by reporters. In the corner, one of the prettiest females Crime ever saw stood holding a child by the arms.

The pretty female that Crime was eyeing had silky black hair that reached down to her lower back. Her slanted eyes gave the look that she had some type of Asian ancestry in her. She saw Mrs. Mary Barton and approached her.

"Excuse me, are you Mrs. Mary?" The girl asked.

"Yes," Mrs. Mary answered to the innocent looking girl.

"Well! Well! I applied for Section 8 Housing for me and my son. I'm a homeless mother and have nowhere to live. My son got sick at the shelter," she said as tears came down her face.

"What's your name?" Mrs. Mary asked the young girl.

"Alesia Gonzales."

"There's not much I can do, until you get your voucher," Mrs. Mary said as she looked at the distraught mother. She knew the girl needed help and was willing to do something for her.

"What type of work skills do you have?"

"I know how to type and answer the phone." Alesia replied.

"Do you know where Bickford Street is?"

"Yes!" Alesia said.

"Meet me at this address," Mrs. Mary said as she passed her a business card.

"Okay." Alesia said as she walked away holding her baby.

Mrs. Mary answered a few questions for the reporters and then led the way, as her family marched out of the courthouse. Greenback held the door open for his mother to step in the limo and then closed the door, the family watched the limo and then left in separate directions.

Mrs. Mary had a meeting at the office with the rest of the Tenant Management Corp. They had interviews to conduct for the security candidates. A few hours into the interviews, they found their security team. They decided to put Robert Connors, a tall, muscular bald headed, ex-security guard as the lieutenant of the security force.

Robert Connors was a Tiny "Zeus" Lister lookalike, with arms the size of tree trunks. He was 35 years old and in the best shape of his life. He shook hands with Mrs. Susan Johnson, Mrs. Mary and the rest of the

Tenant Management Corp. He was excited about his new job and knew that this experience would change his life, but wasn't sure how.

A few days earlier, the Tenant Management Corp bought two Suzuki jeeps that had Bromley-Heath painted in yellow on their side doors. Connors was handed two keys, one to an apartment in the project and the other to the Suzuki Jeep.

"Welcome to the Bromley-Heath Housing Project," Mrs. Mary said, as she smiled at her new head of security.

A light tap on the door, alerted them.

"Come in," Mrs. Susan Johnson said, as she watched Alesia walk in. "Could I help you?" She asked as she looked at the pretty girl holding the baby.

"This is Alesia. She's the new secretary for our security. Could you show her to the office please?" Mrs. Mary asked one of her secretaries.

A chubby girl stepped up and helped Alesia with her baby into the office.

"Alesia." Mrs. Mary called out. "Here are the keys to your apartment and office. Welcome to the Bromley-Heath Housing Project."

Alesia felt blessed that Mrs. Mary gave her a job and an apartment for her and her son Tragdon. "Thank you, Mrs. Mary."

Chapter 6

Alesia walked in the office; a smile emerged on her pretty face. She grabbed the remote and flipped on the flat screen. She turned and walked over toward the business phone that lay on the oak desk. She picked it up and dialed a number. The voice mail came on. She hung up the phone, walked behind the desk and inventoried the expensive furnishing. The desktop computer, printer, fax machine, paper shredder were all going to be put to good use. "I'm going to make the best out of this. Everything happens for a reason."

Outside, in the project, the young kids watched, as the head of the new security force walked around introducing himself. One of the young up and coming gangsters, who was nicknamed "Menace" by the older heads in the project, laughed, as he overheard the security officer assure those listening that Heath Street would be a safe place to live. He knew that nothing would stop the vicious war they were having with the project across the street.

"Toy cop, you can't stop the death toll," Menace said, as he rode past him on his bike.

Robert Connor turned around, looked at the Miami Heat hat that Menace had on backwards and shook his head. He knew there were knuckleheads in the project and vowed to clean up the project as he did previously, when he was named Boston Herald's top security officer for the work, he had done in the Archdale Housing Project in Roslindale. It was the Boston Herald that gave him the name Robo-cop and now he was ready to show the residents of Bromley-Heath Project why that name befit his character.

* * * * * *

The Department of Youth Services van pulled up to the courthouse. Bones, Monster and five other juveniles were handcuffed, shackled and thrown into the van. Monster and Bones carried on a conversation, as others listened. The van pulled up to a juvenile detention center in the Dorchester area of the city. The defendants were marched into the lobby.

Bones sat there while Monster and the rest were brought into the detention center. The reality set in for Bones. He was away from his mother for the first time in his life. He looked at the walls of the detention center and wondered how many times he would see the inside of this building.

"Barton!" An older frail looking staffer named Pops called his name.

Bones snapped out of his thoughts and looked at Pops holding the chains that were going to be wrapped around his waist, wrist and ankles. He stood and raised his arms high. Pops placed the chains around his waist and then locked them. Then he placed shackles on his ankles. Bones was shuffled out the detention center into a waiting station wagon that had a cage separating the front and rear seats. The ride to the Center Point Mental Facility was quiet. Bones looked out the window at the welcome to Tewksbury sign.

"Almost there," Pops said as he took the exit.

Ten minutes later the station wagon passed a string of woods and one thing came to Bones' mind: "Country."

The station wagon turned into a large hospital and stopped at another building that read Center Point Mental Health Facility. Seconds later the door opened, Bones was helped out and escorted into the building. He stepped in the facility. The smell of sickness immediately invaded his nostrils. He hated the smell of hospitals.

They stopped at the front desk. Bones was told to sit down in a plastic chair. Pops passed Bones' court papers to the receptionist and then un-cuffed him.

"Alright Barton," Pops said as he left.

Bones knew his stay was going to be short and he immediately looked for a way to escape.

Chapter 7

Robert "Robo-Cop" Connors wasn't the ordinary security guard. He was fresh home from the war in Iraq and took his job seriously. He was the true definition of a super cop in the past he aided federal, state and local authorities in a successful indictment of the drug dealers in the Archdale Housing Project. Robo-Cop was ignorant of the fact that Bromley-Heath was run by the tenants.

The Bromley-Heath Street Project was considered crime central, as police records credited the project being responsible for 40 percent of the shootings in the city last year.

Robo-Cop walked to his jeep and smiled at the yellow lettering on the side door: "Bromley-Heath Security," he said, as he rubbed his left hand over his bald head. A loud sound speaker snapped him out of his zone. He looked at the source of the noise and spotted a Mercedes Benz wagon parked next to his jeep. The money green Benz was the prettiest car he had ever seen. He watched closely, as a tall dark-skinned man stepped out with a large medallion around his neck. A group of young kids ran up on him and asked for money.

Greenback pulled out a wad of twenty-dollar bills and passed one to each of the little kids. He looked and saw the security guard staring and walked over to the new head of the Bromley-Heath Security. He looked at the jeep, smiled and stuck out his hand.

"Mr. Connors," Greenback said, as he looked down at the shorter security guard.

Robo-Cop noticed the medallion was a Miami-Heat fireball logo in rare red and black diamonds. He took Greenback's hand.

"I'm Greenback. If you haven't heard of me, then you will." He said, as he released his grip.

Robo-Cop felt the power in his hand grip and knew that he was out-matched physically. He looked at the project kingpin who had a smile on his face that showed the diamonds in his platinum teeth.

"I'm Mrs. Mary Barton son, Raymond."

"Nice to meet you," Robo-Cop said as he peeked at the Mercedes wagon.

"I just came to tell you that your job is to keep the senior citizens in the project safe. Leave the kids and the streets to me and don't break the rules because, if you do then that jeep would be swissed."

"Swissed?" Robo-Cop asked, confused.

"Yeah! Swiss cheesed, riddled with holes."

Robo-Cop laughed at the threat. He knew if Greenback attempted to harm him, he would be sent to prison. Robo-Cop felt he was the law but, in all actuality, he was a toy cop.

"You can laugh all you want, just cross the boundary and find out," Greenback said, as he turned and walked toward where the little girls were playing

double-dutch. "OH YEAH, security guard. I'm a man of my word," Greenback said loudly.

"ME TOO," Robo-Cop shouted as his left eye twitched.

"THAT'S GOOD," Greenback shouted as he waved at a few older ladies sitting on their stairs.

"I got a job to do," Robo-Cop mumbled, as he opened the door to his jeep. He sat in the driver seat watching Greenback being saluted throughout the project like he was a celebrity. He hit the sound system and techno music came on. "*Oh, I need some soul music,*" he thought as he hit the gas and reversed out of the project. He pulled into a small plaza on Centre Street that had a Super Stop and Shop grocery store, a clothing store, a pizza parlor and a record store. He parked, hopped out and walked inside the store. He went straight to the greatest hits section and picked out Teddy Pendergrass, Marvin Gaye, Al-Green and Sam Cooke. "These will do," Robo-Cop said. He pulled out his credit card and slid it across the counter.

Menace, Speedy, Juicy and a few other young hoodlums from the project stood outside the pizza parlor talking to a few hood rats. Menace watched Robo-Cop walk out the record store with a bag in his hand.

"TOY COP." Menace yelled.

Robo-Cop heard the young hoodlum and ignored him. He reached in the bag, grabbed the greatest hits of Teddy Pendergrass, took the plastic off it and opened the door. The first thing he did was insert the C.D. into the disc changer and skipped to the song "Greatest Inspiration".

"More like it," he said. Then he turned the volume up.

Menace heard the loud sound of music coming from the jeep. He laughed, as he sat on his mountain bike. He watched the jeep drive by the crowd.

"Fucking soul patrol," he said. He laughed at how comical the new head of security looked.

* * * * * *

Greenback meant what he said to the toy cop. He walked to his mother's office on Bickford Street and used his key to open the door. He stood in the doorway, while his mother talked on the phone. He waited until she finished the call and then sat down in the comfortable chair at the front of her desk.

"Raymond, what's wrong. You look down." Mrs. Mary said.

"The security guard. Who is he? Where did he come from?"

Greenback asked.

"Well I told you at the courthouse that we will have a security force. He is fresh from the military. He was fighting the war in Iraq and his credibility is a plus."

"That's not what I'm talking about."

"What are you talking about then son?"

"Him. I don't like him."

"Why?"

"Because it's a future problem," Greenback said angrily, "I did my homework too. He works with the Feds and the last thing needed in here is a federal investigation."

"Your right, but this memo that I have in front of me, I think you need to look at it," Mrs. Mary said, as she slid the paper across the desk.

Greenback picked up the memo and read it. His eyes got wide. He spotted three of the project buildings that had made the Boston police top ten list of red zone areas: a red zone is a hot spot where a number of shootings have occurred.

"Ma! Think about what you are doing. I would hate to have these little kids out there take out their frustration on Mr. Connors," Greenback pleaded. He rose to his feet, grabbed his mother's hand and kissed it.

Mrs. Mary sat behind her desk and stared at the memo. She hated that her project was targeted as a hotspot. She had met with reporters from the Boston Herald and Boston Globe to let them know that the T.M.C. has made progress attacking crime in the Bromley-Heath Project.

Greenback walked out of the office and stood on the stairs. He watched the same light skinned female he saw at the courthouse a few days ago walking with her son. "Welcome to Boston's worst housing project, there's no project like Bromley-Heath," Greenback said, watching her curvy derriere.

Alesia kept walking. She knew that her body would be a target to all the hustlers in the project and she wasn't going to play herself short. She had a full-time job as a secretary and a full-time job raising her baby. There was no time left to play.

The loud music of Teddy Pendergrass had Greenback searching for the source. His eyes zeroed in on Robo-Cop who was driving into the project, blasting soul music.

"*What the fuck is this guy doing?*" Greenback thought to himself as he stepped off the stairs and posted in front of one of the project buildings that was labeled a red zone area. He shook his head and then walked to the other side of the housing project.

Menace, Speedy and Juicy came over and walked with Greenback to the basketball court.

"When is the next game?" Speedy asked.

"Next weekend we play the Cathedral project, an easy win." Green-back answered, as he heard the loud music again.

"Hey, Speedy, look at the soul patrol," Menace laughed.

"Soul patrol. Where did you get that name from?" Greenback asked.

"Just pay attention to that corny motherfucker," Menace said.

"I can't wait until Alfy gets back out. He's already missed."
Speedy said.

"He's good. He'll be back before anyone knows it,"
Greenback said confidently.

Chapter 8

A gold Mercedes sedan pulled up to Beacon Street and stopped in front of the state house. The backseat passenger stared out the window at the Bulfinch front and then the gold dome. The historic building was like God to the passenger. The chauffeur stepped out and opened the rear door.

Daniel Levi stepped out one shiny shoe at a time. He straightened up his suit, looked at the Boston Commons and said to himself, "what a pretty sight in day time." He knew during the graveyard shift the Commons would be littered with prostitutes, drug addicts and hustlers. He shook off the thought and walked toward the stairs.

Levi was a state representative. He followed closely the articles from various newspapers: The Herald, the Globe, the Metro and the Phoenix. The articles were about violent juveniles but the one that had captured his attention was that of Alfred "Bones" Barton and how he admitted to a murder charge that was dismissed by a juvenile judge.

The articles had different opinions and views from the various journalists. In one poll a vote was presented if juvenile laws should be changed: 63% voted yes, 27% voted no and 10% were undecided. He studied the poll and decided an age limit change was needed for the state of Massachusetts. So, he organized a bill with his legal team and then submitted it formally to the house panel. They studied the law and how this proposed change would affect violent juveniles under the age of thirteen. The panel was content with the wording of the new bill and submitted it to the full House of Representatives. The bill, if passed, would be called the "Barton's Law". It would lower the age limit for violent crimes from fourteen to eleven years old.

The first five days Bones was restricted from using the phone or having visitors. He learned that the evaluation would take 9 months. On his Sixth day the staffer allowed him to use the pay phone. The first phone call he made was to his mother and the next call was to his cousin Crime. He gave Crime the address to the treatment center. He knew that his days were going to get worse and he wasn't trying to stick around for any further evaluations.

"BARTON," The staffer yelled.

"Yo!"

"Recreation time," the staffer yelled.

"How often do we go outside?" Bones asked, wanting to finish his call.

"Every three hours."

Bones watched the staffer turn around and head toward an outside door. He hung up the phone and followed the staffer outside. The sunlight made him squint as he tried to look at the 10-foot fence that surrounded the yard. He searched feverishly for blind spots and found a few. A smile creased his face as he grabbed a basketball and dribbled between his legs. The staffer left the residents alone in the yard.

"*Mistake, mistake.*" Bones thought as he found another blind spot in a corner. "This is sweet. They leave us out here alone, it's like playing hide and go seek in the project. In a few hours I should be back in the project and who would ever think how easy this will be."

* * * * * *

Crime knew where Center Point Mental Residential Adolescent Program was located, when he was an adolescent a female friend he knew was placed there. He cruised Centre Street in a Honda Accord. He had to go and scoop his little cousin up from the program. He took a left onto Columbus Avenue, turned up the volume and blasted the old school B.D.P. song "Criminal Minded"

Bones sat up in his bed and stared at the lone picture of his mother. He grabbed the wallet sized picture, placed it in his pocket and opened the door.

"What time is recreation?" He asked a physician.

"Twenty minutes."

"Thanks."

Bones walked over to the pay phone and dialed his cousin Crime's number. On the third ring he answered.

"Yo!"

"Where are you at?"

"Enroot."

"You know the way, right?"

"Yeah! That shit's in Middlesex County not too far from Lowell."

"Alright, it's in twenty minutes."

"Give yourself ten minutes of leisure then break camp."

"Word." Bones smiled and hung up the phone. He looked at the staff and the physicians and shook his head. "*This is the last time you're going to see my black ass,*" he thought to himself as he walked to the television room, stood in the doorway and shook his head. "Unbelievable," he said sadly.

The juveniles were watching the cartoon Dora the Explorer. He walked away and stared out the window and drifted off. He had a meeting with a Department of Children and Families Agent in a few days and wasn't feeling how the judge stripped him from his mother's care.

"RECREATION TIME." The staffer yelled.

Bones was the first one in line. He walked into the yard and grabbed the basketball. The staffer counted the juveniles in the yard and then walked back inside and locked the door. Bones was relieved they had trust in the juveniles. He shot a few jump shots that hit the rim. He backed up a little further and practiced his long-distance shot. After making 8 out of 12, he tossed the ball. It landed in one of the blind spots. He jogged over to the blind spot and looked to see if anyone was watching and then scaled the fence. He laid down on his stomach and crawled in the grass until he was out of sight. He quickened his pace and rose to his knees and then stood up and took flight. He jogged the rest of the way until the highway became visible. He stopped for a short breather and then hopped over the railing and walked over to the Black Honda Accord his cousin Crime sat in.

Crime spotted his little cousin walking across the street and put the car in drive. Bones walked over to the passenger door, slid in and got low. Crime gave him a pound and then put his foot on the gas and pulled off.

Chapter 9

Greenback was playing an aggressive game of basketball against the Boston Police. Bromley-Heath had a 35 & over team in the (PAL) Police Athletic League. He mimicked his favorite player Moses Malone, giving a series of head fakes and then going up for a monstrous dunk that rattled the rim.

"ARGH, ARGH." He yelled running down the court beating his chest.

Greenback's game came to fame when he was accepted in the METCO program. The METCO program is a grant funded program that allows students in the Boston public school system to attend schools in selected suburbs. METCO is an acronym for Metropolitan Council for Educational Opportunities. It was started in the late 1960s to provide enhanced educational opportunities for participating students, to reduce the racial isolation of suburban school districts and to reduce segregation in the city schools. He was accepted into Newton North and immediately became a star athlete in basketball and football. He took the school to three state championships and two Super Bowls. He had scouts in both basketball and football watching him play. He was the next big thing to come out of Boston, but an inner-city league game sidelined his career. He played for the Bromley-Heath Team and went up for a dunk and landed wrong and tore his ACL. He was forced to sit out his senior season year and watch his scholarships go down the drain. That's when he turned to the street life and never looked back. His opportunity came when most of the drug lords were arrested on a state raid of the housing project and sentenced to lengthy sentences. He picked up where they left off and carried the project on his back.

There was one person who was rumored to be back in the streets that Greenback wanted to show "that he was the man": Jose "Hoop"

Caicedo. Greenback and Hoop battled in everything, but it was Hoop who had the advantage. He had the streets behind him with his brand of heroin that he dubbed "Heart Beat." Hoop was known to tell everyone in the project that he was the heartbeat of Bromley-Heath and, without him, the project won't function properly. Greenback proved him wrong.

Greenback jumped and grabbed a rebound. He dribbled between his legs and then crossed over his defender.

"COAST TO COAST," Lynn yelled from the sidelines.

Greenback floated down the court and passed the ball behind his back to his point guard and went into the paint as the ball came his way. He grabbed it and dunked it. He quickly got back on defense, stole the basketball, passed it behind him with his right hand, caught it with his left and went southpaw for a lay-up.

* * * * * *

The brick buildings of Bromley-Heath came into view. Bones smiled at his project. *"Finally, home."* He thought.

Crime pulled to Centre Street and parked. Bones saw a few of his crew on the bench. He hopped out and walked toward them.

"YO! THERE GO ALFY," Menace shouted, jumping off the bench.

Speedy, Juicy, J.T, Ant Johnson and Menace walked toward Bones and they all took turns hugging him. Crime dapped up Bones' crew and headed toward the basketball court.

"I see you still got them Adidas Torsions on." Menace jokes.

The loud music of Sam Cooke was heard. Bones turned around and saw a blue jeep with the words Bromley-Heath in yellow on the side doors.

"Who the hell is that?" Bones asked.

"That's the soul patrol." Speedy answered.

"Your grandmother tripped out. When you got bagged, she brought security into the bricks," Juicy said.

"That's all that sucker do is ride around and blast soul music." Menace said with venom in his voice, "he calls himself Robo-Cop."

Crime walked over to where Lynn and a few of the Heath Femme Fatale stood near the basketball court. Lynn saw her cousin coming over with a smirk on his face.

"Yo! Lynn, your son's home."

"What," Lynn excitedly said, "I thought he was going to be there for nine months. I see that God is good." She said as she walked away from the basketball court. "Where is he at?"

"He's over on Centre Street."

Lynn marched up to Centre Street with her girls and spotted her son talking to his crew. She walked up and kissed him. "God is good. God is good. I knew you weren't going to be at that place for nine months. What made them release you so early?"

"Ma, I escaped. I wasn't going to spend no nine months in a place like that. Could you believe kids my age and older were watching Dora the Explorer."

"What you mean escape. You kidding right? Or are you just plain ole stupid."

"Neither. I saw a way to leave, so I did."

"Boy, I guess God is not that good today. This boy has lost his mind," Lynn said as she turned to her girls. "I'm going to tell you like your father always told his friends and family. Be safe and remember choices and decisions are made by the best thinkers and you made a stupid choice leaving that place. The first place they are going to come looking for you is here.

Chapter 10

Greenback relished his 36-point, 22 rebound performance against the Boston police, rubbing his skills on the black top in their faces. He stopped at a red light on Columbus Avenue and knew the last shipment of heroin was a little too much for him to handle. He decided to pay his homies at Orchard Park a visit. He took a right onto Dudley Street and cruised until he saw the Orchard Park Housing Project. He drove with the volume low. He hit his blinker, turned into the project and parked on Zeigler Street. He spotted Davey-D and Itchy standing among a group of young project kids with red and black Portland Trailblazers caps on. Greenback left the key in the ignition and hopped out his Audi A-8.

Itchy was the first one to see Greenback pull into the project. He tapped his man Davey-D and they threw their hands in the air. Greenback walked over and saluted the two hustlers with pounds and hugs. He gave the project kids handshakes.

"Itchy, let's take a walk," Greenback motioned with his head.

Itchy excused himself and walked a few feet away from the pack and asked. "What's up?"

"I just got this new shipment of China White and I would match any price that is on the market."

"Name some prices?"

"Two thousand an ounce. It's some good heroin. You could put a five on it, but to be careful, a four is what I prefer."

"I'm ready when you are. Give me a half of a kilo." Itchy answered, scratching his single braids.

"That would cost you 36 thou. Only for you dawg."

"It's all about advancement in this game."

"Exactly." Greenback looked Itchy in the eyes. "I'm all about getting this money dawg, all that other shit is obsolete. If it doesn't make dollars, it doesn't make sense."

"You never lied about that."

They spoke about a few other things and then turned on their heels and walked back toward Greenback's Audi.

"Alright Davey," Greenback threw his fist in the air.

"Alright!" Davey saluted back.

Greenback needed to take a shower and get some head and pussy from one of his servants. He rode through the south end of the city and stopped at a light. His drug connect was breathing heavy on his back and with 800 thousand in the cut he was good. He drove the distance to his penthouse in the Financial District and parked in the underground garage. He took the elevator up to the 22nd floor, stepped off and walked into his palatial. He was greeted by his Swedish house keeper who was in her birthday suit. He used his middle finger to massage her left nipple and told her in the Swedish language to wait in the hot tub. Greenback knew how to speak, write and understand six different languages. He walked further in his penthouse and stopped at the entryway of his gourmet kitchen. He called over his African maid, who was imported from Morocco. He said something to her in her native tongue and watched her disappear. He turned and walked toward the bathroom. He stripped off his sweats and tank top and stepped inside the shower that he called "The Glass House." He washed himself up, stepped out, grabbed a Versace towel and dried off. He made his way to his room and heard the faint sound of his African moaning. He smiled because the timing couldn't have been more perfect. He stepped in the master suite and chuckled to himself. The Swedish house keeper had the Moroccan's legs stretched, as her tongue was darting in and out of her pussy. Greenback massaged his dick and joined the two.

Chapter 11

Greenback's penthouse was located in the Financial District. That's why it cost him 1.2 million dollars. He scored it by the ties he had with the Chinks down in Chinatown. He had strong ties to the Chinese community. It all started in his high school days; he was the star athlete. He was far from the smartest. That title belonged to Cha Ping, a computer genius whose IQ was rumored to be 160. Cha and Greenback became friends and one thing led to another. Greenback was offered a kilo of China White heroin. He declined the first offer, but after the state sweep of his project and a few murders of the remaining hustlers has occurred. He accepted his first kilo of China White and from that day he became known in Boston as Greenback.

Greenback woke up the next morning, to the ringing of his phone. It was his mother who had told him about his nephew escaping from the mental health facility. Greenback couldn't believe what he was hearing and listened to his mother worries, then said his peace and hung up. He had subscriptions to all the city's newspapers and walked to the front door and opened it and picked up his delivery of newspapers. He yawned and walked toward the terrace, flipping through the pages looking for anything relating to his nephews escape, murders, arrests or federal sweeps. He was shocked by the caption: Twelve-year-old Murderer Escapes from the CenterPoint Mental Health Facility."

"This little fucking nigga," Greenback cursed, as he laid the paper down and walked onto his thousand-foot wrap-around terrace. He stared down 22 stories and said to himself, "*I can't believe my nephew. This is not the right timing especially with everything that's going on in my life.*" His vision was fixated on the gold dome of the state house, he wondered what type of activity was going on in there. "*What type of laws, are they trying to pass now?*" He thought.

Unbeknown to Greenback, the law that sat in front of them would affect the way juveniles were treated in the courts. He walked into the large gourmet kitchen and stood near the Sub-Zero fridge, watching his Moroccan maid clean the onyx countertop of the center island. He walked out of the kitchen and into the dining room. He grabbed the remote and turned on the 60-inch flat screen television. He flipped to the local news. His nephew's escape was breaking news. He instantly thought about his younger sister Lynn.

"I have to call her." He shook his head and tossed the remote on the Italian leather sectional and walked into his master suite. The soft powder blue carpet felt like quick sand, as he stomped in the room with his robe open. Next to his California King-size bed was a heart shaped hot tub. Lying on the bed was his Swedish housekeeper, her derriere poked up, as she slept on her stomach. He was staring at his sperm that was floating around in the hot tub from their threesome. He looked up at the crystal chandelier that spun on the 12-foot cathedral ceiling. "All praises due to GOD," he said, as he took off his robe.

Greenback eased himself onto the bed and on top of the housekeeper's sculptured derriere. She inched her derriere up a few inches to allow his manhood in her love box. He was known to put females in submission. It wasn't just his length it was the combination of his length and thickness that made each and every one tap out. He knew what he had was a king cobra dick and he never met a female that could throw it back on him. He rammed his manhood in her from the back. She screamed while speaking a foreign language. He cum rising from his balls, pulled out and squirted all over his Versace sheets.

"Change the sheets," He said, slapping her ass cheek. He stepped off the bed and made his way to the shower. He had to clean up and pay his mother a visit. He knew what his nephew had just done would make the project hotter than it already was. *"I don't need this right now."* He thought.

Chapter 12

Mr. Homicide was furious that Bones had escaped from Center Point. The newspaper article showed how the system once again failed. He summoned Robo-Cop for a meeting at the police headquarters.

Robo-Cop walked in the police headquarters and checked in his gun. He spotted Mr. Homicide pacing back and forth with his arms behind his back. He walked over to the Lieutenant.

"Hey, L.T." Robo-Cop said, as he extended his hand for a shake.

Mr. Homicide pulled his arms from behind his back and gave him a handshake and then walked over to a table and grabbed a stack of papers. "Hang these up on the poles in the project. If you see him, arrest him on sight and call me," He said with authority as he passed Robo-Cop the wanted posters with Bones' face.

Robo-Cop shook his head, as he looked at the wanted posters. "Is there a reward for his capture?" He asked, raising his head.

"Reward! What reward? This little kid has no case pending. He beat the system."

Robo-Cop clutched the posters tightly, turned around and walked out of the headquarters. He looked back and saw Mr. Homicide staring at him. He knew the young kid's escape irritated him. The only thing Robo-Cop wondered was why. "*I wish I never failed that damn police academy,*" Robo-Cop thought.

* * * * * *

Greenback pulled up in his black on black Seven Series BMW. He parked in front of his mother's office. He looked at his blue face Rolex watch and sat in the car for a few minutes. He reached in his pocket and pulled out a knot of twenty bills. He looked at the little kids playing and stepped out. The kids saw Greenback and ran over to him. He handed each kid a twenty, grabbed his key and opened the door to the office.

Mrs. Mary was sitting behind her desk in deep thought. Greenback leaned over the desk, kissed her on the cheek and sat down. She pushed the newspaper toward him.

"I read it." Greenback looked his mother in her eyes. He spotted stress on her face. When his mother stressed it made him stress.

"He has to turn himself in," Mrs. Mary stated. "We can't have him roaming around this project. If he happens to get caught in here, they are going to think we harbored him. I just got a call from the B.H.A. (Boston Housing Authority)."

"What they say?" Greenback asked.

"A lot."

"Did they mention any investigations?"

"No. Raymond, is that all you care about these days?"

"The only thing I care about is life, longevity, your reputation and health."

"Well do what's right," She said, as she turned around and picked up the phone.

Greenback got the picture, rose from his chair and walked out of the office. He blew a kiss to his mother and closed the door. The loud music of Freddie Jackson caught his attention, he turned around and saw Robo-Cop taping a poster on the pole. He walked down the stairs and toward the security guard. "What are you doing?" Greenback asked.

"My job," Robo-Cop replied with his back facing Greenback.

"What I tell you? If you forgot, the streets and kids are mine. Your job is to make sure the senior citizens are protected." Greenback warned as he stared at his nephew mugshot. He reached over, snatched the wanted poster off the pole and ripped it up.

Robo-Cop stared at Greenback like he was crazy. It was just them two in the parking lot. "I got to do my job," He said walking away.

"Next time you violate it's one to the head and five to the body. Just prep your family for what color casket you want to get dressed up in."

Robo-Cop ignored him and kept walking toward the jeep. He knew Greenback was the problem in the project and he wasn't going to take too much of his brash behavior.

Bones, Menace, Speedy and Skitzo were posted outside Juicy's project building, cracking jokes on the benches.

"Yo! There goes the soul patrol." Speedy pointed at the security guard.

Bones stood up letting Robo-Cop see him. The jeep came to a screeching halt. Robo-Cop picked up his phone and called Mr. Homicide, grabbed his handcuffs, opened the door and hopped out.

"ALFRED DON'T RUN, COME HERE." He yelled running toward Bones.

"Oh! Shit," Bones panicked and ran toward the project hallway.

"Don't run, he's a toy cop." Menace advised.

Bones opened the hallway door and ran in. Robo-Cop raced toward the door and caught it before it closed. He saw Bones running up the stairs and pursued him taking two steps at a time.

* * * * * *

Lynn was standing outside the Jackson Square Bus and Train station with the Johnson sisters. The Johnson sisters were named after cars: Porsha, Mercedes, Beema, and Royce. The four sisters and Lynn were part of a girl crew in the project called the "Femme Fatales." Lynn was the face of the girl crew. A MBTA bus pulled up and Alesia stepped off with her son.

"Isn't that the new Spanish girl in the hood?" Mercedes asked.

"Hey." Lynn called Alesia over.

Alesia stopped and turned around. She looked at the girls as they posted in Miami Heat jersey dresses, T-shirts and headbands.

"Come here." Porsha ordered.

The Femme Fatales watched Alesia walk toward them. She stopped in front of Lynn.

"What's up?"

"I see my mother looked out for you with a job and a rent-free apartment." Lynn laughed.

"It was a blessing from God. I needed help."

"Did you meet the girls?"

"No!"

"Well this is Beema, Porsha, Mercedes and Royce and my name is Lynn."

"Hey," Alesia waved at the girls, "my name is Alesia."

"I know. It's Alesia Gonzalez right." Lynn said.

"Yes!"

"How old are you?"

"19."

"There go the jakes," Porsha said pointing at the detectives known as the D-boys.

"They are going to the Old Side of the project." Royce said.

Lynn turned back to Alesia and reached out her hand. Alesia grabbed it and Lynn looked her in the eyes and stated, "You are one of us now."

"I didn't sign up for this."

"Sign up for what?" Mercedes asked.

"To be in a gang."

"A gang. Who said that we are in a gang? This is unification at its finest." Porsha said. "Where's your son's father at?"

"He got murdered."

"Damn! The streets of Boston know how to make a bitch a single mother." Royce said.

* * * * * *

Just as Greenback made his way toward the Old Side two detective cars flew into the project and stopped at one of the red zone buildings. "What the fuck is going on." He said, as he parked on Heath Street.

Bones ran to the third floor and banged on an apartment door. Robo-Cop walked up on him with cuffs in his hand.

"You're under arrest, "Robo-Cop said, as he grabbed Bones and handcuffed him.

"Arrest me now, die later." Bones said.

Robo-Cop laughed at the childish threats and walked him out of the building. As they walked out two detectives were standing there. They took custody of Bones and walked him to a waiting detective car.

Greenback, stood watching from a distance. Robo-Cop had just made his worst mistake. He warned him once and now it was time to send some shots his way. If there was one thing that Greenback honored, it was his word.

Chapter 13

Greenback back peddled and turned around. He couldn't believe the act that Robo-Cop had just pulled.

"Hey, Greenback." Royce waved.

Greenback turned and looked at one of the prettiest females in the project. He smiled and waved back at her.

"Have you seen Lynn?"

"Yeah! She just walked to Centre Street."

"Thanks."

Greenback walked to Centre Street and saw Lynn and a few other girls from the project. They saw him and started to walk in his direction. As he reached them, he looked Lynn in the eyes and said.

"Sis, I need to holler at you." He said motioning his head.

Lynn excused herself from the crew and walked toward Lamartine Street. "What's up bro.? You look kind of concerned is everything alright?"

"No. That new security guard just arrested your son."

"WHAT," Lynn yelled. "He better not had touched my son."

"Yeah! He ran up and arrested him."

"He's going to pay for this." Lynn said with tears in her eyes.

"I got this. Don't worry about it. I warned him and since he didn't follow instructions, he has to face the consequences."

* * * * * *

Bones sat in the back of the police car embarrassed that he had let a toy cop arrest him. He knew once he saw the streets again it was on.

Besides him was one of the worst detectives in Boston. He looked over at the detective and said. "It's nothing they can do to me for I beat that murder charge."

The detective just remained quiet with a smirk on his face. They drove to the police precinct where Mr. Homicide was standing outside. He stopped the unmarked car and opened the door. Mr. Homicide helped Bones out of the car and into the precinct. He was eager to scold the young murderer.

"You thought it was over between me and you?" Mr. Homicide taunted

Bones ignored him and walked into the precinct. The detectives took off one cuff and cuffed his left arm to a wall.

"Call the Department of Youth Services to come and pick him up." Mr. Homicide ordered, as he walked away.

Bones stood with one arm cuffed to the wall. His sole thought was getting at Robo-Cop for playing the superman role.

A half hour later two Department of Youth Services staff: Leroy and Pops walked in with waist, leg and arm chains. Pops looked at Bones and shook his head.

"What's up Pops?"

"Barton!" Pops said, as he waved at Bones.

Mr. Homicide uncuffed Bones and stood back, letting Pops cuff him. Bones looked over Mr. Homicide, as Leroy grabbed his right arm and stuck out his tongue.

Bones was escorted out of the precinct into a waiting station wagon. He looked back at the courthouse that was connected to the precinct and, for the first time, thought about the Judge who had presided over his case.

"Fuck him." Bones concluded.

The ride to the detention center was quiet. Bones thoughts were everywhere. He thought his mother, grandmother, his crew on how they told him not to run and how he wanted to stab the security guard who had arrested him. The station wagon pulled up in the parking lot and they escorted Bones inside of the building. It took fifteen minutes to get Bones situated and escorted up to his unit.

Bones walked inside the unit and proceeded to get his intake done. He wondered if his friend Monster was still there. Once his intake had finished, he was shown his room and then cleared to go inside the television room with the other juveniles. As he walked in, he heard the hood call.

"Oohh, Woohh."

Bones looked around the room and saw Monster throwing up three fingers in the air while he sat in a chair surrounded by other juveniles. In Bones' project the gangsters and the hustlers worshipped Adidas like they were God.

"Bones, my nigga, what you doing here? I thought you were in that nut house." Monster said.

"I was. I saw a chance to slide out and that's what I did." Bones laughed, as he thought about how easy it was to escape from Center Point.

"Yeah! Now, that's what I'm talking about. It seems like you are going to be here for a minute so get comfortable. I have been down for ten months and I run this unit. Welcome to the Thunder dome," Monster said, pushing a Dominican juvenile from Egelston out of his seat. "This is your seat," Monster said, pointing to the now empty seat.

"Who's here?" Bones asked.

"A bunch of nobodies." Monster laughed loudly.

"This nigga's crazy." Bones thought, as he stared around the room.

Chapter 14

Greenback knew if he retaliated right away on Robo-Cop that he would be the prime suspect in what was about to happen to him. So, he waited till the right time and for Robo-Cop to get comfortable inside of the housing project. It took him a couple months to exact revenge and today was the last day that Robo-Cop would ever be seen inside of the housing project.

Greenback finished giving Menace the instructions on how he wanted to carry out the attack on Robo-Cop. Menace listened to him with a smirk on his face. This was the second time in Menace's young life that he clutched a gun. The first was a few months back when he stood on the roof firing off in the air.

Greenback passed Menace the .380 Bryco and told him that once he heard gunshots to assume position. Menace shook his head understanding, and walked toward the alley that he was sure Robo-Cop would drive by. On the roof Juicy stood with a twelve-gauge shotgun. His role was to shoot from the roof into Robo-Cop's jeep so that he would speed forward toward Menace who would shoot at the jeep from the alley. The whole intent was to scare him, not to kill the toy cop.

Fifteen minutes later the loud music of Luther Vandross was heard throughout the project. Juicy stood on the roof with the shotgun pointed, ready to fire. He watched Robo-Cop turn onto Heath Street.

Robo-Cop had the seat reclined back singing loudly "the best things in life are free," he took the turn that would scare him shitless.

"BOOM, BOOM, BOOM." Juicy shot three times.

The buckshot's shattered the front windshield. Robo-Cop ducked and turned the wheel to the left just as Menace stepped out of the alley with the .380 and started firing.

"CLACK, CLACK, CLACK. CLACK."

"OH SHIT!" He yelled, as he pushed his foot harder on the pedal.

Menace stepped back into the alley and came out the other side just as the jeep was flying toward him and fired off the last four shots.

Robo-Cop almost crashed into a lamp post trying to make his escape. He cut the wheel to the right, hopped a sidewalk and skirted out of the project.

Greenback sat on the project bench watching Robo-Cop flee with what he thought was his life. "Hasta la vista baby."

Robo-Cop flew out of the project, turned onto Columbus Avenue, raced through the greenlight, took a left and shot down Cedar Street. He picked up his phone and fumbled with dialing the number. The phone fell out of his hand onto the floor.

"Damn!"

Robo-Cop took a few turns and couldn't believe that shots were being fired at him from multiple angles. He was lucky to escape with his life and knew that his days working security in Bromley-Heath housing project were over. He wasn't chancing his life with odds of getting killed. He saw the Youth Violence Strike Force Gang Unit sign and sighed.

Outside the police precinct Mr. Homicide, Wrinkle Head and Hacksaw Flynn entertained one another with corny jokes. Mr. Homicide looked and saw the Bromley-Heath security jeep speeding toward him.

"Look there goes Connors," Mr. Homicide said pointing to the bullet riddled jeep.

Robo-Cop saw Mr. Homicide, hit the brakes and hopped out. "THEY TRIED TO KILL ME," He yelled, walking swiftly toward the detectives.

Mr. Homicide looked at the windshield that was damaged by the buckshot's and shook his head. *"No respect for security."* He thought. "Come up stairs and write a statement."

Robo-Cop followed Mr. Homicide in the building. His hands shook like leaves as he tried to explain what happened.

"Slow down, we are going to write a report and get to the bottom of this. Are you going back to work?"

"Are you crazy? Have you seen all the bullet holes in that jeep?"

"That's why you failed the police academy, you have no heart," Mr. Homicide laughed.

Hacksaw Flynn came into the room and sat down next to his partner. Hacksaw Flynn tried to hold back his laughter: the frightened look on Robo-Cop's face was comical to him.

"So, you said it was Crime and his brother O-Dawg who did this to you?"

"I don't know no names, I didn't see any faces, all I heard was gunshots coming from the roof and the alley."

Mr. Homicide decided to pin the attack on the two brothers. He wanted to pin it on Greenback, but he knew that the kingpin had his alibi in order and, with his super lawyer, he was sure to beat the case. Mr. Homicide had an indictment pending for after the fact in the murder of Mr. Millionaire. He got a few anonymous tips and grand jury testimonies from recently evicted tenants that the brothers were spotted climbing out of Lynn's window after Mr. Millionaire was murdered.

"We are going to take this statement to the District Attorney office and then wait to get a date for the grand jury," Mr. Homicide stated, waving the statement in the air.

"Whatever it takes, I want someone prosecuted for this."

"I personally would do all I can to destroy the Heath-Mob," Mr. Homicide responded, getting up from the chair. He knew that Greenback was the orchestrator of this attack because of his young nephew being arrested. *"Since I can't get him with this shooting then I'm going to pin it on his nephews."* He thought, as he shook Robo-Cop's hand.

Chapter 15

A few weeks after the incident with Robo-Cop Bones was called into the office and was told that he was designated to Easter Seals in Manchester, New Hampshire. This would be Bones' first time out of the state and he knew he had to play the system to beat them. He packed up all of his clothes, pictures of his family and other important stuff like photos of his favorite basketball players and placed them in two large green plastic bags. He walked into the hallway and over to Monster's door. He peeked in the window and saw Monster laying on his bunk staring at the ceiling.

"Fat boy. I'm out."

"Where are you going to that nut house again?" Monster asked.

"Yeah! Some place called Easter Seals in New Hampshire. I have to do nine months there and then its back to the streets."

"Get through that shit dog and get back to your family and when you see my niggas tell them I'm holding it down."

"Got you my nigga." Bones said, as he walked away from Monster's door and over toward the staff. He picked up his bags and walked with one of the staffers downstairs. He stepped into the receiving area and spotted the one and only "Pops" waiting for him. "Hey, Pops."

Pops saw Bones and shook his head and then smiled. Bones walked over toward him and placed the bags down.

"What's up Barton? Are you ready to get out of here?" Pops asked.

Yup! I'm ready to show the judge I can do this program and that I'm not crazy."

Bones raised his arms high and let Pops wrap the chain around his waist. He snapped the cuffs on his wrist and then applied a black box.

"What's this?"

"The black box."

"Black box, damn this shit is tight. I can't move my wrist."

"It's designed to do that. This is for those who are at high risk to AWOL."

Bones walked out the detention center with Pops. He eased himself into the back of the station wagon and closed his eyes. Pops looked back at Bones and saw that he dozed off.

The ride took 45 minutes to get to Easter Seals. Bones woke up and saw what he thought was an old hospital.

"Damn, this is going to be rough." Bones thought.

Pops opened the door, helped Bones out and escorted him into the facility. Bones sat in a plastic chair. Pops took off the black box and then the shackles. Bones stood up, let him take off the waist chain and then handcuffs.

"Alright Barton! I'll see you in nine months."

Bones sat back down and got ready for the longest nine months of his life.

* * * * * *

While Bones was getting situated in Easter Seals the first indictment came back for Crime & O-Dawg, charging them with "accessory after the fact" in the murder of Mr. Millionaire. Mr. Homicide alerted the local media about the warrant of the two brothers.

Mr. Homicide had the warrant in his hand, as he and three other detectives walked out of the gang unit. "Let's go get them," He smiled, as he spotted the other two cars filled with detectives in the lot. He had his bullet proof vest under his sweater. He walked to the passenger door, opened it and inched his way in. Wrinkle Head put the car in drive and took the back streets until the Bromley-Heath housing project came into view. The three detective cars took different turns into the project.

Mr. Homicide, Wrinkle Head and Fleet Foot took the Centre Street entrance. Hacksaw Flynn, Bobcat Sanders and Bull took the Heath

Street entrance. Wide Face and his partner took an entrance to the Old Side of the housing project.

Mr. Homicide spotted a group hanging outside of 138 Heath Street, He picked up his radio and described his location so that the others could join him.

Crime and a few other Heath-Mob members were outside of his aunt's building hustling. Crime was the first one to see the unmarked police car heading in their direction.

"D-BOYS," He yelled, spinning around and grabbing his waist.

"FREEZE, FREEZE, BOSTON POLICE." Wrinkle Head yelled.

Mr. Homicide saw Crime bolt around the corner. He followed him. Crime pulled out his gun and raced toward one of the project hallways. He heard the detective yell.

"FREEZE, FREEZE."

Crime knew he couldn't let the detective catch him with a gun. He lifted the hood on his sweatshirt, stopped and spun around with the gun aimed.

"BOC! BOC! BOC!" Three shots flowed out of his P89 Ruger.

The first shot hit Mr. Homicide in the chest pushing him backward. He managed to fire off a couple of rounds himself grazing Crime in his leg.

"ARGH." Crime screamed as he hopped to the project building.

Wrinkle Head heard the gunshots, then heard his partner scream over the radio.

"MAN DOWN! MAN DOWN! MAN DOWN!"

Wrinkle Head raced around the corner and saw Mr. Homicide on the ground with his gun in his hand. Mr. Homicide pointed to the hallway that Crime had run into.

Crime made it to the hallway and onto the roof and, with 13 shots left in his handgun, decided to have some fun. He limped to the edge of the roof and pointed the gun at Wrinkle Head who was running toward the hallway.

"BOC! BOC! BOC! BOC! BOC! BOC!"

"That's for my father," Crime mumbled. Those six shots hit the ground inches from Mr. Homicide's head. He covered his head, rolled over and attempted to get up.

The other detectives swarmed the scene as the shots were being fired from the rooftop. Crime backed up, threw his hands high in the air and then bowed to further infuriate the detectives.

"Who's that?" Hacksaw Flynn asked the other detectives.

"It's hard to tell. He had that cone head black hood on," Bobcat Sanders seethed.

Crime knew that the building would be surrounded in a matter of minutes. He backed away, limped to one of his cousin's apartments and grabbed a wig and some women's clothing. He knew what he had to do to make his escape.

* * * * * *

Mrs. Mary was concluding a meeting with the Boston Housing Authority about the newly built Health & Treatment Center. She rose from her desk and shook hands with the representatives. They all walked out of the office. The secretary opened the door. Over 100 SWAT team members in tactical uniforms walked the project with assault rifles in hand.

"What happened?" Mrs. Mary asked one of the residents in the project.

"A police officer was shot on Heath Street."

Mrs. Mary's right hand touched her heart. She looked and saw what looked like an elderly lady pushing a stroller across the lot. She looked closer and saw her grandson Crime's face.

"Oh No! I'm sorry." She turned toward the representatives of Boston Housing Authority.

Crime used the walker to make his escape. He knew if he made it out the project, he was good as gone. He kept pushing the stroller and made it out of the project, caught a taxi to Newton Center and hopped on the trolley. He sat on the trolley in his disguise. He knew that, once he was identified, the search would be on. Where he was headed, he would be safe long as his brother kept it real. He rang the bell, stood up, with his walker got off the train and walked down Commonwealth Avenue. He knew that the project would forever be put under the microscope. He knew what needed to be done, to show the trigger-happy detectives that gangsters shoot back these days. He made it to his hideout, walked onto the driveway, placed the walker to the side and walked up the backstairs into the house. He took off the wig and stepped toward the bathroom to clean off the make-up.

Chapter 16

A few days after the shooting the Mayor, the Boston Police commissioner, police captain and the Superintendent held a meeting at police headquarters. The superintendent requested to have Mr. Homicide restricted from the perimeter of Bromley-Heath housing project. The commissioner agreed. A curfew and a no-trespassing order were assigned to the project. The Mayor requested the Feds to participate in a joint state, local and federal investigation called "Operation Fireball" that would be spearheaded by a hardnosed detective named "Jimbo."

The hustlers in the Academy Homes housing development enjoyed the flood of dope fiends who crossed the street from Bromley-Heath to score their daily fixes.

"I see they are still acting stupid across the street," Uncle Stretch said to his henchman "Broad Day Jay."

"Silliness never pays the bills." Broad Day Jay joked about the uncalled shooting of Mr. Homicide.

"Their loss is our gain," Uncle Stretch answered watching his worker supply the heroin addicts with their dope.

* * * * * *

Greenback sat up in his Penthouse re-counting the money he had stashed. He knew that he spent a lot of money on his lavish habits, but he didn't realize that over 600 thousand was spent. With 400 thousand in the stash, he was close to two million dollars in debt. He thought back to a few months when he counted over a million point five. His problem was spending money on his lifestyle and family lawyer fees. The past few months he had no money coming in because of the violence and the curfew that the Boston police instituted.

"Everything cost," He mumbled.

The fresh shipment of heroin had him in a bind. He had nowhere to move it. The six-day curfew took a toll on his business, as all his customers went elsewhere for their fix. He cursed his nephew for the stupid act he committed on Mr. Homicide. He owed 2 million dollars and counted out only 400 thousand dollars in cash.

"I owe one point six million dollars." He said, as he eased off the bed and walked to the balcony and stared out.

Greenback had to coach a game in the project in a few hours. He walked away from the balcony, into the bathroom, stripped off his clothes and stepped into the shower. He knew the Feds were on their way and his thoughts surrounded the kilos of China white heroin he had yet to move.

"Once I move this, I'm done."

Greenback finished taking a shower and then got dressed and drove toward the project. His thoughts fluttered and this was the first time in his life that he could honestly say that he was stressed out. He pulled up on Centre Street and parked. He stepped out of his car and passed twenty-dollar bills to all the kids who ran up to him. He walked toward his 14 and under team and shook their hands.

"Let's get this win and show the city why Bromley-Heath produce the best talent." Greenback said.

"And gangsters." Menace joked.

The Barton's Law

Chapter 17

A gold Mercedes sedan pulled up to Beacon Street and stopped in front of the state house. The backseat passenger stared out the window at the Bulfinch front and then the gold dome. The historic building was like God to the passenger. The chauffeur stepped out and opened the rear door.

Daniel Levi stepped out one shiny shoe at a time. He straightened up his suit, looked at the Boston Commons and said to himself, "what a pretty sight in day time." He knew during the graveyard shift the Commons would be loitering with prostitutes, drug addicts and hustlers. He shook off the thought and walked toward the stairs.

Levi was a state representative. He followed closely the articles from various newspapers: The Herald, the Globe, the Metro and the Phoenix. The articles were about violent juveniles but the one that had captured his attention was that of Alfred "Bones" Barton and how he admitted to a murder charge that was dismissed by a juvenile judge.

The articles had different opinions and views from the various journalists. In one poll a vote was presented if juvenile laws should be changed: 63% voted yes, 27% voted no and 10% were undecided. He studied the poll and decided an age limit change was needed for the state of Massachusetts. So, he organized a bill with his legal team and then submitted it formally to the house panel. They studied the law and how this proposed change would affect violent juveniles under the age of twelve. The panel was content with the wording of the new bill and submitted it to the full House of Representatives. The bill, if passed, would be called the "Barton's Law". It would lower the age limit for violent crimes from fourteen to eleven years old.

Levi saluted a few state house workers and entered the foyer. He placed his personal belongings on the conveyor belt and walked through the metal detector. He took the elevator up to where the Representatives were to have their meeting. He opened the door, walked into the room and took his designated seat.

Two hours later the state representatives voted unanimously in favor of Levi's bill. Levi rose and shook each representatives hand and knew he was one step closer to changing the way juveniles are charged in the state of Massachusetts. He had two more steps to accomplish: the senate and then the Governor.

* * * * * *

Dr. Leonard Schwartz was an uncle Fester look-alike. His balding hair was cocaine white. His short stubby frame produced short arms. This was Bones' least favorite Psychologist. He diagnosed Bones with ADHD (Attention Deficit Hyperactivity Disorder). He explained to Bones that he had a learning disability with very good concentration.

"The good thing is that you could grow out of this disorder." Dr. Schwartz said to Bones.

Bones remained quiet; he was pissed that he had a disorder. He couldn't wait until his nine-month evaluation was over. He finished listening to the doctor and then asked. "When's my next evaluation?"

"Childhood Disability." The Doctor said.

Bones just shook his head, sideways and walked out of the room. He was escorted to his room by his favorite Psychologist, Dr. Alexander. Bones had an affinity for the doctor. She was a carbon copy of the actress Sanaa Lathan. They resembled each other's pretty facial features, medium frame and hair length. They could easily pass as twins.

"What's wrong Barton?" She asked.

"Nothing," Bones replied with his head down.

"Make sure you stay practicing basketball against that ghost," Dr. Alexander joked.

Bones laughed and looked at the pretty doctor. She constantly teased him about the ghost. Bones spent his leisure time practicing his ball handling skills and shot selection with a nerf ball. She caught him one day playing against his shadow and from that day forward teased him. Bones had six months left of evaluations. He knew what he was going to do when he hit the streets. He planned on getting revenge on the security officer who had arrested him.

Chapter 18

Jose "Hoop" Caicedo was the only Colombian to hail from the Bromley-Heath project. During his peak in the drug game he was arrested, tried, convicted and sentenced to serve a 7 to 9-year state sentence. While he was paying his debt to society, he kept his ear to the street and what he kept hearing was the name Greenback. Hoop was a man of class. He never had a jealous or envious bone in his body, but in his eyes some people deserved to have it all while others did not. The problem he had with Greenback was the lack of homage that he should have paid to his forefathers. Hoop was against the project wars. He was strictly about unification. After all, he was the founder of the Heath-Mob Syndicate.

Hoop completed his state sentence and returned back to the project. He walked into the courtyard and noticed all the Miami Heat memorabilia. "What the fuck? We in Miami?" He joked, walking toward Heath Street.

"Hoop, welcome home," A few older ladies waved, as they sat on their stairs braiding hair.

"I'm glad to be back," He answered.

Hoop heard loud music, as he neared the basketball court. He came closer, slowed his pace and watched Greenback coaching the project 14 and under team. Hoop's yellow skin turned red, as he saw Greenback coaching the league, he founded ten years ago.

The Maria Caicedo league was a city youth league that Hoop founded. He named it in memory of his late mother. Greenback eventually became commissioner and renamed the league the Mary Barton City League.

In the 70s the Bromley-Heath housing project included three separate projects: Bromley Park, Heath Street and Bickford Street. The three projects sat on three acres of land and had three activists as the heads of each project. They decided to come together and form a management corporation which they named "Tenant Management." That was the start of the three projects merging into one. They contracted with B.H.A. (Boston Housing Authority) to perform management functions for the project.

Maria Caicedo managed the Heath Street side of the project. Mrs. Susan Johnson managed the Bickford side and Mrs. Mary Barton managed the Bromley-Park side of the project. Mrs. Mary Barton eventually became the executive director, a position that was supposed to go to Mrs. Caicedo. A renovation sparked off and the buildings on the Bromley-Park side were upgraded while the Heath Street side remained in ruins. This infuriated Mrs. Caicedo. A year later Mrs. Caicedo stepped down and vacated her post as project activist. Her children saw their mother go from an activist to a hermit, a state in which she eventually passed away years later. Her son Jose learned from the doctor that his mother had died from stress. He blamed the Tenant Management Corp for her untimely death. This was where he and Greenback had their disagreements.

Since their youth, they battled in everything from basketball, football, hustling and even project leadership. When Greenback got injured and was forced to sit out his senior season. Hoop took his team, Newton South High School, to the state championship and won the title. Greenback sat back and watched Hoop garner all the attention in the media. The win was an insult to not only Greenback, but also to his team Newton North, because Newton South was their #1 rival. The scouts flocked to Hoop and sent dozens of letters of intent, but the money he was making in the streets was his pride and joy. He bi-passed college for a P.H.D in street pharmaceuticals.

Hoop, along with Natho, Six-Nine, Face, Lizard and P-Boy formed a syndicate of hustlers on the Heath Street side of the project called the Heath-Street Mob. They allied with Jay-Jay, Larry Taylor, Essie Johnson and his brother Terry who called themselves the Bromley-Heath

Syndicate. With a common understanding, they joined together to form the Heath-Mob Syndicate.

The Syndicate controlled the flow of heroin, marijuana and cocaine in the project. Greenback, then known by his government name "Raymond" was on the outside looking in. Hoop refused to call him what everybody else called him. He knew him as Raymond and Raymond only.

Hoop watched all the younger Heath-Mob praise Greenback, like he was some hero. He walked over to where the females stood watching the game and palmed one of their asses.

"What the fuck!" Mercedes said, as she jumped and turned around. "Hoop?" She said, excited to see one of the project top hustlers.

Lynn turned around when she heard the name Hoop. She was oblivious to the friction that their families had in the past. She had a crush on the light skinned Al-B Sure look alike ever since she was a little girl.

Hoop looked at Alesia in her red tennis skirt and gave her a thumbs up. He looked at Lynn and knew he remembered her but couldn't connect the face with a name. He went from her face to her thick thighs and hips. She saw his wandering eyes and turned sideways to watch the game.

"Who's that?" Hoop asked Mercedes.

"That's Lynn Barton, Greenback's little sister."

"Damn!"

Greenback saw Hoop and came among the crowd. He looked down on the shorter Hoop and smiled.

"Jose, long time no see. Welcome home," Greenback said, extending his hand.

"Always a pleasure to meet a man like you, Raymond," Hoop responded, grabbing his hand.

Lynn looked at the two and wondered why they were on a first name basis. She looked at her brother's smirk and knew something was up, but as long as it didn't affect her, she was cool.

"The Bromley-Heath Street basketball team is the best in the city. We outshined Orchard Park, Mission Hill Project, Columbia Point

Project and any other project or team in the city. It comes from good coaching," Greenback bragged tooting his own horn.

"That's good to hear Raymond. This project always breeds talent."

"I know it does, Jose, it was nice seeing you and, once again, welcome home. There's a spot in the mob if you want it, but remember there's only one boss in Heath and his name is Greenback." He said as he turned and walked away.

Hoop stood there, embarrassed at how Greenback had talked down on him. After a few seconds of deep thought, he walked away his thoughts were cluttered and knew he had to get back in position. Hoop decided to take a trip for a few months down south to speak to his Colombian family members about some Afghanistan heroin. He knew if he was able to get his hands on some of that heroin that all the money in the project would be coming to him.

"Let's see who gets the last laugh," Hoop giggled, walking away.

"Who's that?" The federal agent asked the detective Jimbo.

"That's Jose Caicedo. His street name is Hoop."

"Is he a major player?"

"Was a major player. He just got out of prison."

"State or fed?"

"State."

"Is he on our target list?"

"Now he is." Jimbo smiled.

Hoop walked past a half of dozen parked cruisers on his way to Centre Street. *"Damn, Crime made it hot as hell out here."* He thought as he found a bench and sat down. He thought about all his former crew who were either locked up or dead, he knew in order to take over the project the way he wanted he needed to find the next wave of hustlers. He didn't care if he had to divide the project into two, then he would do it for the satisfaction of his mother. He knew with all the police presence in the project he had to disappear until the heat died down. He was sure that a federal indictment was on its way. *"Too much gunplay brings the feds."* He thought. "I'm going to Miami to establish myself for a few months. I'll see you when I get back Raymond, I hope you're ready," he said getting up from the bench and walking toward his rental car.

* * * * * *

Menace was dancing with the basketball, as he dribbled between his legs. His defender reached, Menace crossed him over and went in for a lay-up, only to pass it to Speedy who straddled the three-point line. Speedy grabbed the ball and shot it.

"NETS!" Lynn yelled, as the shot hit the bottom of the nets.

Greenback paced back and forth. He was pissed that Hoop made his return back to the project. He knew that was competition and the timing was not good. He was indebted to his Chinese connection and his nephew Crime made it hot to be in the project. That was two bad things.

"Bad things come in threes. What's next, a federal indictment?" He mumbled.

The Heath-Mob team won by 17 points. Greenback took his team to the local pizza parlor. He ordered 4 large boxes of cheese pizza and called Menace to the side.

"When we leave, you and Juicy are coming with me. We are going to get those fireball tattoos."

Menace face lit up. He finally was going to be able to show the world that he was a Bromley-Heath representative.

"I'm ready now." Menace said.

"Not him," Greenback pointed to Juicy, who was sitting and devouring a large pizza.

"I guess not." Menace laughed.

It took Juicy no time to finish the pizza. Menace walked over to the table and tapped it.

"Come on we have to go."

Juicy got up and waddled outside to where Greenback stood in front of his Mercedes wagon. Menace took the passenger seat while Juicy took the whole rear seat.

Greenback hit the air conditioner and put the car in drive. They drove to Cape Cod and pulled into a small tattoo parlor parking lot. They stepped out and Greenback was saluted by a few artists who stood outside smoking cigarettes. Greenback pointed to two chairs. Menace and Juicy took their seats.

"You could get it two places, either on your neck or between your thumb and index finger." Greenback explained.

"I want mine on my neck." Menace said.

"I want mine on my hand." Juicy answered.

Greenback passed a logo to each artist, as they came into the shop. He reached in his pocket, pulled out a knot and handed them a couple twenty-dollar bills. Half hour later the artist was applying alcohol over Menace's fresh tat. Menace hopped up, cocked his neck to the side and examined the fireball.

"More like it," Menace shook his head and walked toward Greenback. "I'm ready to show the world that I'm Heath-Mob affiliated."

Greenback dropped them both off at Jackson Square and pulled off. He pulled beside a black Seven Series BMW and looked at the dark tints. He knew the car well. It belonged to Uncle Stretch, the Godfather of Academy Homes.

"*Sucker,*" Greenback thought, as he switched lanes. He made a U-turn and decided to relax at one of the businesses he had in Hyde Square. He drove a short distance, pulled in front of his cleaners and parked.

"I need to relax and figure out my next move." He said, popping the locks.

Chapter 19

The Senate approved Representative Levi bill and passed it on to the Governor for his signature to make it law. It took the Governor less than six hours to study and sign it, making the Barton Law effective. From this day forward any juvenile as young as eleven years old could be charged under Levi's Law.

The remaining months flew by for Bones. He packed up and was transferred back to the detention center to wait for his court date. He walked in the unit and heard Monster's deep voice yell.

"Eight-ball, left corner pocket."

Bones kept stepping toward his room. He placed the bags on the floor and then joined the other juveniles in the game room.

"BONES. I see your back from that nut house."

"I'm back." Bones said, as he started to tell Monster about his experience in Easter Seals. He left out the part that he was diagnosed with ADHD.

"All I keep hearing in the streets is how big your uncle Greenback is doing."

"That's his thing, he does it and does it big," Bones bragged about his uncle Greenback's flamboyant lifestyle.

Bones waited till Monster finished his game of pool and then they both walked inside of the television room and sat down. A few minutes later a staffer walked in the room with a DVD in his hand.

"What's that?" Harm asked.

"SOUTH CENTRAL." The staffer yelled, inserting the disk into the DVD drive.

All the juveniles in the room sat quiet and watched the movie. Bones liked the way little J-Rock banged the deuce. He knew that he and J-Rock were one in the same, both relentless. An hour into the movie a new juvenile arrived in the unit and his appearance in the juvenile system was perhaps the most high-profile case in the state of Massachusetts.

That new juvenile was Shyheim "Scar" Carter. He was the first case of the new Barton Law. He was accused of murdering his cousin. At Twelve years old Scar was the youngest ever in the history of Massachusetts to be charged for a homicide.

While the juveniles in the detention center were watching South Central, Scar was in the hallway getting his intake done. He was named Scar for the nasty pear-shaped Scar on his left cheek. He finished his intake and was allowed to enter the television room.

The staffer flicked the light on and took the DVD out. Minutes later Scar came bopping into the room with an Atlanta Braves T-shirt on. He spotted an empty seat next to Bones and sat down. Bones looked over at the little kid and wondered why he was in prison.

"Yo! Where are you from?" Bones asked.

"Academy Homes," Scar answered.

"SMACK." Bones slapped Scar out of his seat. He stood over Scar and backhanded him. "HEATH STREET, HEATH STREET." Bones yelled.

Scar tried to fight back but was too small for the stronger Bones. The staff came into the room and a staffer named Crazy Danny leaped in the air, tackled Bones to the ground and pulled his arm upward.

Scar was picked up by another staffer and escorted out the television room. The look on Scar's face showed it wasn't over.

Bones was rushed to the cool-off room. He knew that from this day forward every time he saw Scar that they would have some sort of problem. He paced in the room for a couple hours. A staffer came to the door.

"BARTON."

"What?"

"You have court tomorrow."

Bones sat up all night in deep sweat. He knew that he was going to have a strong family presence. He just needed all of the doctors to give him good reports. The thought of the power that his grandmother had in the city put a smile on his face. The only thing he wanted was to be back in his mother's custody. His hands were clasped behind his head with his eyes closed. It would only be a matter of time before the snoring came. He hoped that the judge would rule in his favor and send him home to his mother instead of placing him in the foster care system. What Bones didn't know was that the new law they had passed was named after him and that from the day that the law was passed the juvenile justice system would never be the same.

Seven o'clock came faster than he expected. He heard the staff doing count. He hopped up and sat on the edge of the bed. This was his day to see if they would grant his wish.

"BARTON! COURT!" A staffer yelled.

Bones stood at the door waiting for Monster to walk by. Monster was the last in line because of his height. Monster stopped and told Bones that he would see him on the streets. Bones nodded, sat back down and waited his turn.

A staffer opened the door and passed Bones a bag that had two honey nut cheerios, a boiled egg, apple, orange juice and a carton of milk. Bones devoured the breakfast and then dropped to the floor and banged out twenty push-ups. He hopped to his feet and heard the door opening.

"Barton," A staffer called.

Bones was escorted out of the hallway and into the gym. He knew that there was going to be a few other people going to court also. He walked into the gym and saw a little over a dozen other juveniles, dressed and ready to go to their respective courts. Bones walked to the corner and sat on a blue mat, studying at one person in particular. This person had on a Cincinnati Reds T-shirt, white sweat pants and a pair of white Adidas Forums. Bones took it as he was from Castlegate Road.

Castlegate Road was a side street in the Grove Hall area of the city. This was a place that Bones was unfamiliar with. He knew that gang mostly wore Cincinnati Reds memorabilia. He looked at the curly haired gangster then focused on the sheriff officers who came in with fist full of chains.

"ROXBURY COURT! BARTON, DAVIS, JONES AND SMITH." The sheriff officer shouted.

Bones and the one he assumed was from Castlegate walked up. Bones was handcuffed with the black box and shackled. He noticed the one from Castlegate also had a black box. They were escorted to the sheriff's van and when the latches opened Bones heard a voice shout out.

"Who's that Quamie?"

Bones hopped inside the van and sat down next to another juvenile. He listened as the others jockeyed Quamie. Bones learned a lot during the short ride. He learned that Quamie was indeed from Castlegate and that he was on a firearm charge. The ride was short to Roxbury Court. The sheriff took all the juveniles out of the van and escorted them in-side the courthouse and into an empty cell. Bones sat on a bench and closed his eyes and started to get the rest that he never had gotten the night before.

Chapter 20

Mr. Homicide returned from his eight months leave and sat at a table in the Youth Violence Strike Force gang unit with a few other detectives that included a black detective named Brett Jones.

Brett Jones was the most recent detective to get cross deputized as a federal D.E.A. agent. He would be used to buy heroin from the dealers in the Bromley-Heath housing project.

Mr. Homicide looked at his watch and said: "It's about that time." The detectives minus Brett Jones stepped up and walked towards the door. "Greenback is the #1 target on the microscope," Mr. Homicide said looking at Brett Jones.

* * * * * *

Bones felt a hand shaking him. He opened his eyes and saw Quamie's face. Bones flinched.

"Your name Barton?"

"Yeah! Why?"

"COURT," the court officer shouted through the bars.

"What type of mood is he in?" Another juvenile asked.

"A good one. He freed two out of three so far," The court officer said.

"Word." The juvenile pumped his fist.

Bones got up off the bench and stretched. He walked over and placed his arms between the bars. He was handcuffed and escorted past a string of cells, stopping at a door.

Mr. Homicide and a few of his partners walked into the courtroom. Mr. Homicide was the only one out of the three smiling. His smile was more of a laugh now, cry later. He vowed to get back at the Barton family for their attempt on his life.

Lynn, Greenback, Clarence and Terrence looked at Mr. Homicide and all busted out laughing. Mr. Homicide retained his smile and found a seat on the opposite side of the courtroom. The door opened and Lynn saw her son being escorted by a court officer and seated inside of a booth.

"Baby, I love you." Lynn said, as she waved at her son.

Bones sat in the booth as the court officers took off his handcuffs. After the cuffs were taken off, he looked back and blew a kiss to his mother and waved at the rest of his family. He looked at the spectators inside the courtroom and saw that it was packed with detectives, doctors, family members and friends. Dr. Alexander made Bones smile, as he saw how sexy she looked in her beige pants suit.

"He's in a good mood," Bones' lawyer whispered in his ear.

"ALL RISE." The bailiff shouted.

The whole courtroom stood while Judge Black came out of his chambers and walked to his seat on the bench.

"All may be seated."

The district attorney was the first to give his opening statement. He explained how Bones was a danger to society, how he escaped from Center Point shortly after his arrival. He called Bones a child with a teenager mind state. He explained to the judge that he had witnesses from Center Point. Bones' lawyer, Mrs. Curran, sat there with her legs crossed, taking notes. He finished his opening statement with the words "Alfred Barton is more than a danger to society; he is a murderer who beat the system."

Mrs. Curran rose out of her seat and walked up to the center of the courtroom. She looked at the judge and said: "Good morning your honor, how has your day been going so far?"

"Good, very good Mrs. Curran. Thank you for asking."

"Your welcome, your honor." Mrs. Curran said as she cleared her throat and took a quick sip of water. "This is not a complicated matter we are facing today. It's a rather simple one that should have one result.

A Twelve-year-old as a danger to society, is ludicrous, to say in the lamest term. This Twelve-year-old sitting in front of you is Alfred Barton, the grandson of one of the top activists in the city of Boston. My client Alfred Barton is the Twelve-year-old child of his mother Evelyn Barton. He committed the crime, he was accused of and ordered by the court to be evaluated at a mental health facility. There is clearly nothing wrong with this young child. He panicked for the first time in his life being taken away from his mother. He did what he felt was best and that was to walk away from the facility. He knew what he did was wrong and completed the nine-month evaluation at the Easter Seals Mental Health Facility in Manchester, New Hampshire. There are psychologists, school teachers and family here today to testify that he has no mental issues." Mrs. Curran finished her opening statement and sat next to Bones.

"That's a true one-hundred-thousand-dollar lawyer." Greenback whispered to Lynn.

The first person to take the stand was Bones' mother. Then his grandmother, school teachers and then the chief psychologists Samantha Rubenstein. She reached the stand and looked at the crowd. After being sworn in she began to explain that Bones was an active, athletic child with an average intellectual ability. She broke down how his attention and concentration skills were similar to those of an average kid. In his first month she explained that he had behavioral issues which was common with kids being stripped from their natural habitat. Dr. Rubenstein finished up by giving the court Bones' intellectual profile. She explained that his verbal IQ was 103, his performance IQ was 106 and his full-scale IQ was 104. She opined that his numbers placed him in a good range.

Next was Bones' least favorite, Dr. Leonard Schwartz. Dr. Schwartz explained to the court that he evaluated Bones during his first month at the mental institution. During this testing, he found that Bones had ADHD (Attention-Deficit-Hyper-Disorder) and a quick temper that included negative behavior. He looked down at his notes and explained that during Bones' second month, his temper had gotten better and his ADHD was starting to improve. He stated that Bones was an active child, whose only down moments came when he couldn't reach his mother on the phone.

Bones looked at his mother and smiled. Lynn blew her son a kiss and pointed to her heart. Bones watched as Dr. Schwartz stepped off the stand. Next was his clinical psychologist, Dr. Alexander. Butterflies swarmed in Bones' stomach, as he sat up and watched his favorite doctor take the stand. Dr. Alexander started off with the story of how she found Bones playing basketball with his shadow and then went on to how his cognitive functioning was above normal. She also stated that her mental evaluation was compatible with Dr. Schwartz's: Bones improvement in the ADHD department. After she was finished a few other psychologists gave their reports and then the chief psychologists came back to the stand to conclude the findings. She summarized in a few words that Bones had no mental health issues, that his mood and social abilities were normal and that he was athletic, goal orientated and coherent. Dr. Rubenstein requested that Bones be placed back in the care of his mother.

Mrs. Curran stepped up and gave her closing statement. "Your honor, you heard from the various psychologists, family members and school teachers. There are eighty-five hundred children in the department of Children and Families custody and they are exposed to severe potential harm." The courtroom remained quiet as Mrs. Curran gave her closing statement. "The foster care system exposes our youth to severe potential harm. I need to reiterate! The foster care system exposes our youth to severe potential harm. There's been many reports of abuse and neglect by the foster care parents. Many of our children languish for years without permanent placement and some even age out. There's only one result here, your honor." Mrs. Curran looked at the judge, backed up and sat down.

The District Attorney gave his short speech and sat down. He knew the judge was going to free Bones. The judge looked through a few pages on his desk and was ready to give his verdict.

"I have reached my judgement, ladies and gentlemen. I reverse my previous judgement and place Alfred Barton back in the care of his mother, Evelyn Barton. Court is adjourned." He banged his gavel and disappeared into his chamber.

Chapter 21

The whole courtroom erupted in applause, as the judge banged his gavel. Bones reached and hugged his lawyer. Lynn ran up to her son and hugged and kissed him. Bones hugged his grandmother, his aunt Lena and gave pounds to his uncles.

Mr. Homicide watched the hugs and kisses from the back of the courtroom that Bones was getting from family members. *"Unbelievable."* He thought.

Bones looked at Mr. Homicide with evil in his eyes. Looking at the look on Mr. Homicide's face was when Bones realized that he had beat the system. He watched the detectives walk out of the courtroom. Dr. Alexander came and gave Bones a hug.

"Take care and pursue your dreams of playing basketball," Dr. Alexander said, giving Bones a light kiss on the cheek.

Alesia and the Johnson sisters were outside in the lobby. The door opened: Lynn and Bones stepped out. Alesia smiled, showing her dimples, as Bones walked toward them. Lynn stopped and introduced the two.

"Alfred, this is Alesia. Alesia this is my son Alfred."

"Nice to meet you. I heard a lot about you bad boy," Alesia smiled.

"I see you in the project. I have to take my son shopping and to get something to eat."

Alesia saw a look in Bones' eyes that she never saw in anyone his age. He looked like he was possessed by the devil.

Lynn walked out of the courthouse. Bones was a few steps behind her. He saw a shiny yellow Five Series BMW in the parking lot. The sound of the doors unlocking told him that his mother came up. He opened the passenger door and slid in. The smell of Black Ice air fresh-eners filled his nostrils. Lynn pulled out of the parking lot and into a traffic jam. She maneuvered through the jam and switched lanes.

"Damn! There they go," Lynn cursed.

Bones inched his body up and stared into the window of the black Seven Series BMW. Both occupants had red and blue Atlanta Braves hats on their heads. Bones noticed the passenger had the coldest look on his face.

"Who's that?" Bones asked his mother.

"That's the supposed to be Godfather of Academy Homes, Uncle Stretch and his trigger man, Broad Day Jay," Lynn answered.

Bones heard a lot about the two from the rival project. He wondered whether Uncle Stretch had more influence and money than his uncle Greenback. He looked over at his mother: Do Uncle Stretch have more money than my uncle Greenback?"

"Hell no! Greenback is the man." Lynn said, as she maneuvered out of the traffic jam and stopped at a sneaker store called Alpha & Omega in Dudley Square. A navy-blue Mercedes pulled up alongside them. "There he goes." Lynn said with a smile on her face.

Bones noticed his mother having become excited like a little kid on Christmas and wondered why. "Who's that?"

"My boyfriend Maser."

"Boyfriend."

"Yeah, my man," Lynn smiled, opening the door.

Bones watched, as his mother hugged the curly haired Dominican. He watched his mother point toward the passenger seat. Bones opened the door, stepped out and walked toward them.

"What's up little man," Maser said in broken English.

"What the fuck? This nigga using my mother for a stash house," Bones thought as he realized that Maser was Dominican. "What's up?" Bones said, as he gave Maser a handshake.

Maser grabbed Lynn's head and kissed her on the lips. Bones' adrenaline pumped, as he looked on the ground for a broken bottle or a stick to put in work: Maser had no business kissing his mom. Maser reached in the back seat and passed Lynn a shoe box and spoke to her in Spanish. She nodded her head and placed it in the trunk. Lynn said something in Spanish and in a flash, Maser reached in his pocket and passed her some money. She put the money in her purse, kissed him one last time and walked into the sneaker store with her son.

"When you learn Spanish?"

"A few months ago, Maser taught me."

Bones knew then and there that Maser had been in his mother's life for some time. "Do you love him?"

"Yes. I love him and very deeply. But this day is not about me and Maser, it's about you. I'm so happy that you are back home with me."

Bones couldn't believe that his mother fell in love so fast and he felt like her love was fading fast for his father and he needed to get her to come to her senses.

Chapter 22

Alesia made it to the project after she picked up her son from day-care. She walked past Menace, Juicy, and Speedy and waved at them. Menace blew a kiss in return.

"She is the prettiest girl in the project." Menace said looking at how beautiful Alesia was.

"That's perfection." Speedy lusted.

Alesia walked to her office and opened the door. She had to do some clerical work for Mrs. Mary. This was her first-time seeing Bones eye to eye and she felt a chill run up her spine. The look in his eyes was that of the devil. She sat down in her office and cut on the computer.

Menace watched Lynn's yellow BMW pull into the lot. He motioned his crew and they stood on the benches.

"YO! THERE GOES ALFY." Menace shouted, as he saw the passenger door open.

Bones stepped out of the BMW and saw his crew standing on the benches. He threw his hands high in the air and ran toward them. Menace hopped off the bench and met Bones midway in the lot. They hugged like long lost brothers.

"Hi, Lynn." Menace said hugging her.

"Make sure he stays out of trouble."

Menace ignored her and walked away with Bones. "Yo! Guess what?"

"What." Bones said.

"We got hammers now," Menace said proudly.

"Word, where are they at?"

"On the roof."

"The roof," Bones stated confused.

"Yeah, rooftop. They call us the Rooftop Boys. From the high rise we could see all the way into Academy Homes."

They walked to the benches where Juicy and Speedy waited. Bones hugged his boys and inquired more about the guns.

"What kind of guns?"

"A rifle, a three-eighty and a three-five seven with a body on it."

"A body? What do you mean a body?" Bones asked.

"Yeah! Your cousin Castro murked a nigga the other day near English High." Menace informed.

"English high. The high school?"

"Yeah! We were down there starting trouble and he saw a chain that he wanted and one thing led to another." Menace smiled.

Skitzo came toward the crew with a brown paper bag in his hand. He approached the crowd. "Poppa got a brand-new bag." He smiled and passed the bag to Menace. "Welcome home Alfy."

"Thanks dawg, but I prefer the name Bones."

Menace looked at Bones and laughed. "Nigga, your name is Alfy around here." Menace said, as he pulled out a .9mm Browning out of the bag and passed it to Speedy. Next he pulled out a .380 Taurus and tucked it in his waist. Then he passed the bag to Bones. "It seems like we are starting to get a lot of guns."

Bones reached in the bag and pulled out a shiny .38 Special with a black rubber grip.

"They can't trace revolvers if you get rid of the shells." Skitzo informed, watching Bones admire the new handgun.

"Let's take a walk down Centre Street." Bones said, as he placed the gun in his waist.

"Naw, let's go up on the roof and let these bad boys off at the passing cars." Menace said.

"Are you crazy?" Speedy said, "Anyone could get hit."

Menace thought about what Speedy had said and agreed shooting at passing cars was unsafe. Bones started to slowly walk away followed by his crew. As they walked to Centre Street a heroin addict walked up to Juicy with crumpled up money in his hand.

"You working?" the heroin addict asked, looking sketchy.

"Yeah." Juicy said as he reached in his pocket and pulled out a bag of heroin and passed it to the addict. The addict grabbed the heroin from Juicy, turned around and took flight. "YOOOO!" Juicy yelled.

Bones first reaction was to catch the addict and beat him up. He was too slow for the speedy addict who sprinted through the project like Carl Lewis so he stopped, reached in his waist and pulled out his handgun. He aimed and pulled the trigger twice.

"POW. POW."

The addict fell to the ground and Bones and his crew ran in the opposite direction. They made it to a hallway on Heath Street and Bones passed the gun to his crew and walked outside of the building toward the other side of the housing project.

Alesia was in her office when she heard two gunshots. She ducked and then looked out of the window. She saw Bones sprint past her office window with a gun in his hand.

"I know he didn't," Alesia said as she saw someone on the ground trying to crawl to safety. She backed away from the window and sat down. *"Too much goes on in this project, I don't know if I should continue living here."* She thought.

* * * * * *

Greenback was pulling into the parking lot when he heard two gunshots. He parked, reached in his waist and pulled out his .357 automatic handgun. He saw his nephew Bones run through the project with a gun in his hand.

"What's this kid up to?" Greenback thought, as he backed up and drove off. He took another entrance inside the project one that would lead him to his sister Lynn's apartment building. He put the gun in his waist and got out of the car. He walked swiftly through the housing

project and saw the Rooftop Boys posted outside of a project building. He looked for his nephew and saw that he wasn't among the crowd. "Where is Alfy at?"

"He went to the other side of the project." Menace informed. "You want me to go and find him?"

"Nah, I got this." Greenback said as he walked to the other side of the project and saw his nephew sitting on a set of benches outside of Jackson Square. From a distance Greenback heard the sound of police sirens. "ALFRED." Greenback yelled, "GET YOUR ASS OVER HERE." He said angrily.

Bones walked over to his uncle and sensed that his uncle was angry. "What's up uncle?"

"Come with me." Greenback said, as they walked to where his car was parked. They got in the Audi and sped off. "You must have lost your mind. I came here today to congratulate you on coming home to be with your mother and you went and done some dumb shit. Don't say you didn't do it or shoot any gun because after I heard the shots, I saw you run with a gun in your hand. You must be stupid or really belong in that nut house."

Bones' feelings were hurt at how his uncle had talked to him. He couldn't believe his uncle had spoken to him in such a harsh manner. *"He doesn't even know what happened?"* Bones thought. "You're yelling at me and don't even know what happened. The fiend tried to beat Juicy and I started to chase him and couldn't catch him so I just pulled out the gun and fired two times to scare him. I don't even know if he had even gotten shot."

"Whether he did or didn't that was some stupid shit. I know one thing. You better hope he didn't get shot or you will be in trouble."

"I hope not too." Bones thought, as he sat in the passenger side staring out of the window. He saw the gold dome to the state house and wondered where they were going. "Where are we going?"

"To my house." Greenback said as he pulled up and parked in his designated parking space. He opened the door and stepped out. Bones followed him to the elevator.

The elevator stopped on the 22nd floor and Bones stepped off and into a spacious penthouse. Bones noticed that his uncle had an extremely beautiful housekeeper cleaning up. *"Damn, my uncle is the man amongst men."* Bones thought, as he followed his uncle through the house. *"Millionaire dreams."* Bones said to himself, as he watched as his uncle stared at a picture of his whole family at one of their family reunions.

Without looking at Bones, Greenback said nonchalantly. "Come and sit-down Alfred. We need to talk." He said as he led the way to a suede sectional couch. He sat down, reached in his pocket and pulled out a wad of cash. "Welcome home." He said, as he passed him the wad of money. "I don't take lightly senseless violence in the project. It's one thing to protect yourself, but it's another thing to bring unnecessary heat to the project. When senseless violence happens in the bricks it falls down on me, my money and my mother's reputation. It's a lose-lose situation for all of us. I saw you running through the project earlier with the gun in your hand and if I saw you imagine how many others saw the same thing. I don't know what comes out of this mess you have created, but for the meantime I'm keeping you close to me and in doors until we find out what's what."

"Okay." Was all Bones had managed to say. He agreed with his uncle that his reckless behavior was bad for the family. He knew better than to follow behind anyone and vowed to never be a follower again.

Chapter 23

The next three months Bones had laid low at his uncle's house. He thought a lot about the shooting and believed if they ever had brought charges against him, they could not hold him because of his young age. He watched as his uncle walked inside the room with a confused look on his face.

"What's up uncle, is everything alright?"

"We have to talk." Greenback said, as he sat down next to his nephew on the sectional. "I just spoke to your mother and she told me the detectives came by her house with a warrant for your arrest for that shooting."

"A warrant. You kidding me right." Bones said, as he saw the seriousness in his uncle's face.,

"Nah. They are looking for you. I need to call my lawyer and talk to her to see what she may be able to do for you." Greenback said as he pulled out his phone and dialed his lawyer's number. The lawyer answered on the second ring and Greenback spoke to her for a few minutes and then hung up. He looked at his nephew and said. "She told me that they had created a new law after you called "The Barton's Law" and the law is designed to charge juveniles young as eleven for violent crimes."

Bones whole insides felt funny. He couldn't believe what his uncle had just told him. He knew that his uncle was telling the truth because he was not known to lie to anyone. With the thought of spending months or even years in the juvenile system made Bones resent what he had done.

"So, what's next?" Bones asked.

"We have to meet Mrs. Curran tomorrow morning at the police precinct so that you can turn yourself in. I don't know what is going to happen but if you get a bail, I will be there to come get you. Your moms will be over here in a few to spend some time with you."

Bones nodded his head and slouched backward onto the sectional. He knew he could handle any time in the juvenile system, but if he had known about the new law then he would have thought twice about pulling the trigger.

Twenty minutes later Bones moms arrived and they spent the rest of the day talking and eating. After the conversations he had with his moms he felt more at ease and was ready to see what evidence the court had on him.

The next morning Greenback drove Bones to the police precinct. Mrs. Curran was in the lobby waiting. She saw Greenback and Bones walk in and ran to them.

"You're in trouble," She pointed to Bones. "They have a lot of anonymous witness accounts of the shooting and the best I can do is try to get you a plea deal."

Two uniformed police officers came from out of the back. Bones hugged his uncle and shook Mrs. Curran's hand. He knew this one was going to be different from what he had experienced in the mental health facility.

"I see you when this is over." Bones said to Greenback as he was handcuffed by the two police officers. After they finished cuffing him, he walked away with them. He was booked, finger printed and had his mug shot taken. Next he was escorted to a small holding cell. "*I can't believe I'm going through this.*" Bones thought as he found a spot on a wooden bench, curled up and dozed off.

An hour later Bones was awoken by the cell door opening. He sat up and saw two police officers standing there. He jumped off the bench and walked over toward them and was escorted upstairs to the court-house. He was placed in a cell with five other juveniles. It felt like a blast from the past. He couldn't believe that Quamie from Castlegate was inside the cell going to court. A couple hours later a court officer came to the cell and shouted.

"BARTON, COURT."

Bones was taken out of the cell and escorted to the courtroom. He walked inside the courtroom and stood next to his lawyer. The courtroom only had a few members of his family.

"ALL RISE." The bailiff shouted.

The judge came out of his chamber and took his seat on the bench. He looked at the docket sheet and shook his head. He lifted his head and looked at Bones with an evil stare.

"ALL MAY BE SEATED."

Bones sat down; his knees were shaking under the table. He knew the streets of Boston wouldn't see him in years. A tear fell down his face. He looked back at his family members in the courtroom and shook his head. The next fifteen minutes Bones listened to his lawyer present how he was the alleged shooter to the judge and he didn't like how the district attorney painted him as if he was a hardened criminal.

The judge listened to both arguments and decided to give Bones no bail and remand him to the custody of the Department of Youth Services. Hearing the words remand would forever sit in Bones' mind. He knew this was the beginning of a chapter of his life that would make or break him. He stood up and allowed the court officers to handcuff him. He heard the muffle of his mother's tears and knew that she was shedding tears for the love that she had as his mother. He didn't bother to look back as he was escorted to a holding cell.

Chapter 24

The Ping On triad was the iron hand that ran the heroin, cocaine, prostitution and illegal gambling in Boston's Chinatown. The leader of the Ping On was Kwok Ping, a well-dressed, well spoken, genius. He was the one who masterminded shipments of China white heroin into the state of Massachusetts. He set up operations in the south and north shores sections of Massachusetts. He used Boston as his home.

Kwok met Greenback through his son Cha and offered Greenback a kilo of China white. Greenback declined the offer, but then later on accepted. For collateral he had to give his mother's personal information and a few addresses of his kids. Greenback knew Kwok had power, but didn't understand how much power he actually had.

Greenback pulled up to his cleaners and sat in the car for a few minutes. His phone buzzed. He looked at the screen saver and saw it was his Chinese contact. He answered it.

The chink on the phone told Greenback that they needed to have a meeting and to bring the cash that he had for Kwok. Greenback put the car in drive and pulled off. It's been two months since his nephew Bones was sent to the Department of Youth Services. In that time period he had sold three of his seven businesses and from the sale of the businesses he accumulated five hundred and eighty thousand dollars. He knew this meeting could go anyway and, never the one to put his mother in harm's way, he agreed to attend. Within no time he pulled up to his penthouse and parked. He took the elevator to his floor and stepped off. He opened the door and hit the combination to his secret wall safe, took the money out and placed stacks into the money counters. He rubber banded each in a ten thousand stack and placed them neatly in a duffel bag. He left 30 thousand in the safe. With all the heat that the project now had thanks to his nephews he was down close to 1.5 million dollars. He took off his black Patek Philippe watch, pinky ring and diamond chain with the Miami Heat logo, three sets of car keys and titles to his remaining businesses and his homes. He walked into the dining room and called his mother. He got the voicemail.

"Ma! I love you." He said before he hung up. He picked up the duffel bag and took the elevator downstairs and placed it in the passenger seat of a nondescript car.

Chinatown was walking distance from where he lived in Beacon Hill. He pulled up to Tyler Street, parked and waited. Ten minutes later a tap on the door spooked him. He jumped, rolled down his window and passed the bag to the courier. The courier disappeared through an alley. Greenback put the car in drive, as he went to pull off a motorcycle zoomed down the street and cut him off. Greenbacks eyes grew wide, as he saw a submachine gun pointed at him. He tried to duck, but his reflexes were too late. The .45 Uzi peppered his upper body, neck and face. The gunman continued shooting for the next fifteen seconds.

The hit was placed on Greenback from Kwok Ping, the leader of the Ping On triads for being a bad business partner. The hit was more to send a message to Greenback and others about the dangers of being a bad businessman and not a man of his word.

"When it came to business, it was business." These were the words that Kwok Ping lived by.

* * * * * *

Hoop made his way back into the city. He had three uncut kilos of Afghanistan heroin. The heroin was strong enough to put a ten on it, but he told his cook crew to make seven kilos out of one. Hoop was ready to take the heroin to a few of the city housing projects before he made his way back to his own housing project.

"I'm going to make this six-project tour and then come back home and lock it down."

Hoop had plans to deliver heroin to Maverick Project in East Boston, Old Colony Project in South Boston, South Street Project in Jamaica Plain, Franklin Field Project in Dorchester, Bunker Hill Housing

Project in Charlestown and Lenox Street Project in the Southend. These were the six projects in which he had direct contact with the top hustlers. Hoop sat back and waited his turn. When it came, he would give Greenback the no mercy rule. What he didn't know was that Greenback had just gotten murdered and that the project was now in his hands.

Chapter 25

The Boston Police Homicide unit had Tyler Street cordoned off in yellow caution tape. The detective Mr. Homicide had Greenback's phone in his hand. He felt the phone buzz, looked at the screen saver and read the text that Greenback's mother had sent saying that she loved him.

"There's no use in calling the ambulance, this guy's dead?" Mr. Homicide smirked. "Notify Mrs. Mary and tell her that her son's number came up." He said to one of his fellow detectives.

Lynn and Lena were on their way to their mother's office when a police cruiser drove past them. They stopped for a second and then kept walking forward.

"Look, they are going to Ma's office." Lena pointed.

"For what?" Lynn asked, as they kept moving forward.

Mrs. Mary opened the door to the two uniformed police officers. The officers were there to inform her of Greenback's death. Mrs. Mary clutched her chest and leaned on the door.

Lynn looked at her mother talking to the officers and watched, as she clutched her chest and leaned on the door. "OH! SHIT!" Lynn shouted and ran toward her mother.

The officers turned around quickly as Lynn and Lena ran up on them.

"What's going on?" Lena asked.

"No! Baby, Raymond is dead. My Raymond is dead." Mrs. Mary cried.

Menace stood on the roof and watched the officers approach the office of Mrs. Mary. He watched closely as his thoughts became confused at how emotional they had become. He decided to join them out front. He left the roof and walked up to the sisters and asked. "What's wrong?"

"My brother Raymond is dead." Lynn cried.

"What?" Menace asked.

"Someone killed my brother," Lena said angrily, hugging her mother.

Menace backed up and walked away. He couldn't believe that the expiration date for the boss of the Heath Mob had come. He knew who was next up for the crown, but if he didn't get his fair share, he would make it hard. The only reason Menace didn't make it hard for Greenback was because he was kin to his best friend Bones.

* * * * *

Hoop sat in his brand new triple black seven series BMW with a female he had just met. His phone buzzed. He looked at his screen saver and saw that it was his man Lazy. He answered it. He lowered his head to the news that Lazy had just delivered. He never wished death upon anyone and for it to happen to Greenback put him in a position to either restructure the Heath Mob or let them go into ruins. He knew his next move was going to be big and it would put him in the eyes of everyone in Bromley-Heath as the king.

Hoop made a few more calls and confirmed that Greenback was indeed dead. He pulled off and drove straight to Casket Royal. He parked and hopped out, He bopped into the shop and stopped at the front desk. Hoop smiled at the receptionist who was a carbon copy of the actress Jessica Beal.

"May I help you?" The receptionist asked.

"I would like to order a custom-made casket."

"What kind do you have in mind sir?"

"I would like to know if y'all could make a custom casket in the shape of a car."

"Yes! We could, what kind of car are we talking about?"

"A Bentley Azure."

"Yes! We could order the custom grille and add tires sir."

"I would also like the steering wheel made with hundred-dollar bills and flashing headlights."

"How you would like the body positioned sir."

"Upward with his hands clutching the steering wheel."

"Like he's actually driving?"

"Yes."

"I need to know the body weight and height of the deceased?"

"Around six foot five and 250ish."

"It's going to cost you thirty thousand dollars."

Hoop pulled out a stack of money and counted out ten thousand dollars and slid the money across the counter.

"That's a down payment."

"Could you fill out this paper?" The receptionist asked, as she looked into Hoop brown eyes.

Hoop saw the look in the pretty receptionist eyes. He smiled showing his dimples as he started to fill out the paper with Mrs. Mary's address and phone number. He finished and walked back to his car. He opened the door and sat in the driver seat in deep thought for a few minutes. He put the car in drive and pulled off. He fished up the nearest train station and pulled out a knot of twenty-dollar bills and passed her five. "The train is waiting for you."

"What!" The female stated with an attitude.

"You heard me, hop on the train," He said pushing her out of the car.

"Fuck you Hoop." The female rolled her eyes.

Hoop watched as she got out of the car and pulled off. He needed to study the atmosphere of the project, but before he did any research he had to go and pay his respect to the Barton family. It took him ten minutes to reach the project. He pulled up into the parking lot, circled the lot and parked next to a yellow BMW. He sat in the car for the next ten minutes shaking his head, as he watched crowds of people in tears. He pulled out his phone and dialed his man from New York who specialized in painting murals.

"Yo! What's up son?"

"I need a favor. One of my friends was murdered and I need you to come down to Boston before the services and paint a mural in the project," Hoop demanded.

"Got you son. Anything else? E-mail me the picture and the description and I'll be down there in a few days,"

"Alright got you."

Hoop hung up the phone, opened the door, stepped out and walked toward Mrs. Mary's apartment.

Outside of Mrs. Mary's apartment was over two hundred people in tears. The first person to spot Hoop coming was Royce. She pointed to her sister Mercedes and they both got excited.

Hoop walked up and kissed each female on the hand and offered his condolences to each family member. He walked up to Lena, grabbed her hand and kissed it.

"Hey Jose."

This was Lena's first-time seeing Hoop since he was arrested nine years ago. Her eyes were bloodshot red from crying.

"I send my condolences to your family for the loss of a genuine, good man. I definitely express my gratitude and tell Mrs. Mary that his casket has been paid for. That's the least I could do for your family."

"Thanks Jose."

"Always," Hoop said, as he walked away.

Lynn was standing on her mother's stairs watching Hoop talk to her older sister. She hoped that his return back to the project would be permanent. She watched him walk away, turned and stepped inside of her mother's apartment. It's been a couple weeks since she had broken up with Dominican Maser and now the man, she always lusted for was back in the project. There was nothing that would stop her from making Hoop her man.

Chapter 26

Greenback's funeral was held at Morning Star Baptist church in Mattapan, Massachusetts. The wait to view the body was an hour long. The line stretched down Blue Hill Avenue and around the corner to Morton Street. Over a thousand people flooded the church parking lot and Blue Hill Ave, paying their last respect to the boss of the Heath Mob.

Hoop was stuck in a traffic jam as he navigated his BMW down Blue Hill Avenue. He took a left and parked on a side street. He stepped out, walked to the corner and admired the massive crowd outside the church. He counted the city blocks leading down to the church and made his way.

"Damn! This shit is high profile," Hoop said, as he spotted a few news vans, reporters and a half of dozen unmarked detective cars. He made his way to the front of the church, stopped and greeted a few Heath Femme Fatales who had on R.I.P. Greenback shirts. He hugged each one of them and then made his way inside the church. He stood in the doorway and stared at Greenback's six-five frame propped up with his hands on the steering wheel. His black straw hat was tilted to the side showing his wavy hair. The red and black silk shirt and linen pants showed he was a man of style. *"The game doesn't stop till the casket drops."* Hoop smiled.

Lynn saw Hoop staring, so she got out of her seat and walked toward him. She wanted to show her appreciation for making her brother's wake memorable. "Thank you," She said, stopping in front of Hoop.

"It's no need for a thank you, I did what a real one is supposed to do." Hoop said, as he gave Lynn a hug and walked toward Mrs. Mary. He reached her and gave her a kiss. "I send my condolences to you and your whole family."

"Thank you, Jose."

Hoop turned around, looked at the casket and smiled. He did his due's burying the former kingpin in style.

Menace watched Hoop closely from the back of the church. He knew it was Hoop's turn to take control of the drug traffic in the project. *"As long as he feeds the wolves there won't be any problems."* He thought.

Hoop attended the service for a half hour and then walked out of the church. He spotted Itchy and his Orchard Park crew walking his way. Hoop reached out his hand for dap.

"What's up Hoop. I was doing my numbers with Greenback. I know you are about your business and when you get back look me up. I be on the Bumps all day dawg."

"You know where to find me. I will be on Centre Street from this day forward." Hoop said.

"Okay. I have forty thousand I owe the nigga Greenback in this bag. I'm going to give it to his mother so that she can pass it on to his kids." Itchy said holding up a Louis Vuitton drawstring bag. "I was shocked when I got the news about his passing because we had made plans for future moves, but hey that's why you live every day like it's your last cause bullets have no names."

"Hey Hoop," A female voice said.

Hoop heard his name called and turned around and saw it was one of the Johnson sisters. He saw Porsha walking over toward him. She reached him and gave him a hug.

"Hold on Porsha. Itch, we're going to link. Let me just get my shit in order and I will be down the Bumps to holler at you."

"Okay dawg." Itch said as he gave Hoops a pound and a hug.

Hoop watched Itchy and his crew walk inside the church and then he turned to Porsha. ""This is crazy that we are out here mourning the loss of Raymond. But life must go on. You know I'm all about my money. There's a new landlord in the project and I'm doing things differently. I'm giving out cash incentives, performance bonuses and amenities. Spread the word."

"I'm down." Porsha said, giving him another hug.

They spoke for a minute or so before they were interrupted by her little brother Menace. Porsha excused herself to allow them two to talk.

"What's up dawg?" Hoop said, looking Menace in the eyes.

"I hope you feed the wolves, since the crown is yours."

"What type of food the wolves eat." Hoop jokes.

"Money." Menace said sternly.

"I'm feeding all the wolves. With me, it's an equal opportunity, for I don't believe in 'I eat first then the others eat."

Menace knew that was a low blow to Greenback's ideology of him eating first then feeding the wolves last. He looked at Hoop and hoped he was a man of his word. "I hope so," he said as he turned around and walked away.

Hoop just managed to smile at the young up and coming gangster. He walked to his car and decided to drive around the city until the repast started. After two hours of driving around aimlessly he drove to the project and pulled up in Plant Court. He parked and made his way through the project. He spotted a few young girls from the Barton Clan walking with pans of food.

"Hey, Hoop?" Myami said, waving.

"What's up? If I'm not mistaking your Raymond's daughter?"

"Yes. I'm Myami one of the twins."

"Once again I send my condolences out to the family."

"Thank you." Myami said."

Hoop walked to the parking lot and leaned on a pole. He watched a few cars pull up and park. A half of a dozen members of the Heath Mob joined him in the lot. He greeted each with a pound and a hug.

"I guess the ball is in your court dawg," Red hawk Taylor said.

"Nah! This is for everyone, not just me. When I eat my niggas eat."

"I hope so. I don't mean to speak ill of the dead, but the nigga Greenback was for dolo and check this, he only had thirty thousand to his name," Lazy said.

"Who told you that?" Spanish Dan asked.

"I overheard Lena telling the twins."

"Damn! Thirty stacks that's it. He had to have some money buried somewhere." Red hawk shook his head.

"He was good for the kids but as far as us, his niggas, if we aren't working for him, then we had nothing coming. He was a good nigga, but a selfish one too." Lazy barked.

"Whatever you want to do Hoop, I'm rolling." Spanish Dan reached out his hand for a pound.

Hoop sat back and ingested how Greenback's legacy was damn near in ruins by his selfish behavior. He now understood what Menace meant by feeding the wolves. He looked and saw Lynn coming across the lot with a cooler in her arms. Her twin brothers were with her.

"Damn! Lynn is looking better as she ages," Spanish Dan said.

"Don't play yourself. That's my cousin Alfred's baby mother." Lazy reminded Spanish Dan.

Lynn spotted the Heath Mob and waved at them. The twins stopped and gave pounds to everyone.

"Yo! Could I holler at you?" Clarence asked as he stopped a few feet from Hoop.

Hoop and Clarence walked away from the group and stopped next to a black Honda Accord. "Thanks for burying my brother in style. He deserved to be buried like a boss. If you need me or my brother for anything let me know. We are here at your disposal." Clarence said, as he hugged Hoop.

"The Heath Mob shall continue. How could we have a Heath with no Bartons?" Hoop smiled.

"Exactly." Clarence said, returning a smile. "Come on, let's go get some of my family's soul food and celebrate my brother's death."

They walked back to the crowd and then over toward Bromley Hall where the repast was being held. They entered the hall and Hoop saw Menace standing with Juicy, Speedy and Skitzo and Bone's Cousin Castro.

"He said he is going to feed the wolves." Menace said to his crew.

A Heath Mob member named Crook walked over to Hoop and pulled him to the side. He looked Hoop in his eyes and said: "I've been hearing whispers that Lynn is trying to get at you. I want you to know from a gee to a gee that her son is a murderer."

"So am I," Hoop responded seriously

Chapter 27

After Bones was convicted, he was committed to the Department of Youth Services to his twenty first birthday. He learned at his staffing that he was designated to serve his time at the long term R.F.K. (Robert F. Kennedy) Secure Treatment Center in Westborough, Massachusetts. He started off his tour in the juvenile justice system as a trouble starter. In his first 24 months he accumulated a total of 17 fist fights, three assaults of staff and was placed on the R.F.K. Secure Treatment's shit list. He constantly stayed on the entry level.

The Entry level was the lowest level possible. While on entry level Bones was stripped of all his privileges: television, radio, leisure time and store runs. Being stripped of playing basketball made Bones get his act together. Basketball was his stress reliever and within two years he got his act all the way together and made it to the highest level and became a model prisoner. After 4 years of being held captive in R.F.K. he was transferred to Braintree, Massachusetts to participate in a residential program.

The director of the program was Mr. Thibodeau. He was a hardnosed director who took no shit from any juvenile, white, black or Hispanic. His reputation consisted of kicking juveniles out of his program and sending them to the harshest secure treatment center that was located in Westborough, Massachusetts. He also helped those who were willing to listen to him and follow his strict rules. Once they reached their levels, he awarded them with outside trips to the movie theater, local bowling alley and roller-skating rinks.

The day that Bones walked into the program, Mr. Thibodeau saw how big he was and knew instantly that Bones was a man-child. He knew a basketball star when he saw one. He watched Bones closely, when he saw him play basketball, he knew Bones was the savior he needed.

During Bones' years in the Department of Youth Services he sprouted several inches to six foot five and weighed a solid 220 pounds.

Mr. Thibodeau was the basketball coach for Braintree high. He watched year after year as other schools in his conference dominated and took home titles in the division and the state. He knew that Braintree was one or two big players away from getting the chance of lifting the trophy in the air. He offered Bones an opportunity that was never offered to anyone in the history of the program. He offered Bones enrollment into the nearby Braintree high school. Bones knew by accepting the offer it would give him the experience and exposure he needed to take his game to the next level. He accepted and became the team's starting power forward.

Bones was sitting in his room watching television when a light knock on his door made him look.

"Barton mail," the staffer said, passing Bones a piece of mail. Bones was sick of all the recruitment letters front the local colleges. He still had his senior year of high school and he was already flooded with letters from New England's top colleges. Other than recruitment letters, mail was foreign to him. He and his mother had not spoken since he learned that his cousin Crime was arrested, convicted and sentenced to 50 years for the shooting of Mr. Homicide. He grabbed the letter and looked at the post mark in the upper right-hand corner. "*Manchester, New Hampshire.*" He thought it was a recruitment letter from a small college. He opened the letter and read it.

"*Dear Alfred,*

I know this is a surprise for you to hear from your favorite psychologist. I was saddened and disappointed the day you were arrested. The years that you spent in the Justice System will either make or break you and I see that it made you a better man (smile). I have been following your basketball career and I see playing against the ghost paid off (Lol).

I no longer work at Easter Seals. I have my own mental health center, here in Manchester. Alfred, achieve your goals and dreams no matter what obstacles get in your way. Leave your emotions at the door.

Sincerely,

Dr. Alexander (Sanaa Lathan) ...

P.S. I will see you at the championship..."

Bones re-read the letter six times. He couldn't believe his luck. He thought about her often during the past years. He got off of the bed, picked up his ball and walked into the hallway. He spotted the director at the desk. "Mr. T, what time are we going to the YMCA?"

"Soon as the van comes back."

"Alright, thank you," Bones said, as he walked out into the small yard and practiced on his jump shot."

Bones led the state of Massachusetts in scoring with 36 points per game and was second in rebounds. He took his skills to another level when he played in front of hundreds of people. They nicknamed him the "Crowd Pleaser."

Bones walked outside and tossed the ball toward the backboard and grabbed it for a two-handed slam. Slam dunking came easy and natural to Bones. At 6'5" he had the wingspan of a 6'9 forward and a 40" vertical. Bones practiced every day leading up to the big game. He went through drills of passing to his teammates, mastering his jump shot and slashing to the hoop. He was pretty much set on defense. He averaged 6 steals and 4 blocks per game. As he waited for his ride to the YMCA, he was busy setting up his 15, 17- and 19-foot jump shots. He was automatic when it came to the 17-footer. This was what Bones liked the most about his game, his deep threat presence. He was hyped to learn that his mother and grandmother would be attending the game to support him. Bones knew it wasn't going to be no walk in the park. His team was playing against the defending 3-time state champions, Avon High.

Avon High had the twin towers: The McLaughlin twin brothers. The twins were heavily scouted by every division one program in the nation.

Avon's average margin of victory was 28 points per game leading up to the championship.

"I'm going to show why they call me the crowd pleaser. I'm going to put up sixty in this game."

Chapter 28

The image Hoop carved in the city in the past six years left him untouched. He dodged the stick-up kids, police investigations and other enemies. The streets no longer called him Hoop. He was now known as the "Commissioner".

The Commissioner's run in the streets was as long as that of any successful hustler who graced the inner-city of Boston. With his direct pipeline of heroin from his family in Bogota, Colombia, he was able to supply 17 of the city housing projects with top quality dope. He was doing so good that he was able to make Bromley-Heath a safe environment for kids. He ceased all the violence and entertained all the senior citizens' needs and supported Mrs. Mary's wishes. In the past six years the violence that once plagued Bromley-Heath was now a thing of the past. Mrs. Mary was awarded resident of the year and recently opened a grocery store across the street from the project. One of the first things he did was stop all of the heroin and crack from coming into the project. The only thing he allowed to be sold in the project was marijuana. Every month he brought 100 pounds of mid-grade marijuana and passed it to the Heath Femme Fatales, flooding the project. He stationed his Heath Mob members to the other projects he controlled and opened up a few heroin houses up the street from Bromley-Heath. His plans left no reason for the F.B.I. to spark any investigation into Bromley-Heath.

The Commissioner's money was flexible as he was able to give-away turkeys to the unfortunate families in the projects for Thanksgiving. For Christmas he rented U-Haul trucks and spent a couple hundred thousand on toys for the under-privileged kids. In his eyes education was important. He made sure all the kids who received good grades were awarded with a hundred dollars for each A and fifty dollars for each B on their report cards. He became the top hustler in the city, superseding Uncle Stretch from Academy Homes, Charlie Hustle from the Hole, Nice from Castlegate and Casino Mike from Theodore Street.

His heroin reached the shores of South Boston where he delivered, set up shop and controlled all the traffic in Old Harbor, D-Street and Old Colony housing projects. He had Archdale and Beech Street housing project in Roslindale. East Boston's Maverick and Orient Height were two of his money makers. He still had dope running through the veins of the junkies in the Bunker Hill housing project in Charlestown.

He made his rounds and found a nice little heroin operation in Brighton's two housing projects, Faneuil and Fidelis Way. Because of his good relationship with the gangsters in four of Roxbury's housing projects he gave low prices to the top hustlers in Lenox Street, Orchard Park, and Mission Hill and Ruggels Project. The only project he was able to supply in Dorchester was the Franklin Field housing project. The Southend families welcomed him with his brand of dope. He had hustlers running in and out of the Cathedral Project and Villa Victoria. The only projects he didn't have direct contact with were Franklin Hill and Academy Homes. He knew gaining entrance in those two projects would create a war zone. Those were the areas that Uncle Stretch, the Godfather of Academy Homes controlled.

Lynn went along for the ride with her man. She traded in her yellow five series BMW for a purple Mercedes CL63 with egg shell interior and chrome wheels. She was on top of her game and so was he. There wasn't much that either could ask for.

Lynn and Hoop were in Natick, Massachusetts at New England's biggest mall: Natick Collection. She was shopping at Louis Vuitton for a blouse and sandals. She was ready to show how flamboyant she lived at her son's championship game. Lynn was proud that her son found basketball as his savior from the streets. She was living too much of the good life to have him ruin it. It was bad enough that he ruined this attempt once in the past.

Hoop rented a yellow school bus for all the project kids and parents to show support for Bones. He wanted to show Bones that, whatever he wanted to do, he was there to support him 100%.

When the wolves feel like they weren't getting a fair share of the pie emotions start to form. It was Menace's emotions that Hoop wasn't ready to deal with.

"I can't wait to see my son take down the nets." Lynn said excitedly.

"He reminds me of Bromley-Heath's best player Greg "Smooth" Simpson when he was doing his thing for Madison Park." Hoop said.

"I'm rolling with my son, he's the best I ever saw next to my late brother Greenback."

"Cut it out. Smooth is the best that Bromley-Heath ever saw." Hoop said. After hearing the name Greenback, it made Hoop quiet, he knew if it wasn't for his untimely death, he wouldn't be in the position that he was in. "You like this?" He changed the subject as he held up a bell bottom cat suit.

"Yeah!"

"Good because this is what you are wearing."

Hoop finished the rest of their four-hour shopping spree in the mall. Lynn was in love with Hoop and she wasn't going to let no one spoil her happiness.

Chapter 29

The Massachusetts state championship game was held at Boston's T.D. Bank Garden. The Garden was packed. The top two high school teams were set to duel it out for the state title.

Avon high was looking to capture its fourth consecutive title while Braintree was out for its first title since 1969. Bones and his teammates formed a lay-up line. He watched the Twin Towers shoot jump shots.

"Overrated," Bones snarled.

Lynn, Hoop, Alesia, The Johnson sisters, Mrs. Mary and over three dozen family members and friends walked toward their seats. Lynn looked onto the floor and saw her son. "There he goes," Lynn said excitedly.

Hoop looked at Bones and saw how enormous he had become since the last time he had seen him. "*Damn, that little nigga got gigantic.*"

Scattered around the Garden were scouts from all the top Division 1 colleges: Georgetown, Syracuse, Connecticut, Pittsburgh, Kansas, Kentucky, Boston College, Duke, Seton Hall, and Virginia." They were there to watch the McLaughlin brothers while other smaller programs like U-Mass, Babson College, University of New Hampshire, University of Maine, Boston University and the University of Providence were there to watch Bones.

Dr. Alexander walked in with her daughter who was a splitting image of her. The only difference was the color of her daughter's eye color. She had hazel eyes. Her daughter's hair was pulled back in a ponytail that reached the right of her breast.

Brad and Chad McLaughlin were practicing 19-footer jump shots. Brad walked to half court for the tip off. The referee threw the ball into the air and Avon won the tip off. The ball was taken by their point guard. Bones came up to play his tenacious defense, waving his hands in front of his opponent. The point guard attempted to cross over Bones and was stripped. Bones grabbed the loose ball and raced down the court. Bones stopped, dribbled between his legs, crossed over a defender, tossed the ball to the backboard, caught it in the air and reverse dunked it. He held on to the rim as the crowd went crazy. He hopped down, looked at the crowd and threw up an H with his fingers for his project.

"THAT'S MY BOY." Lynn yelled.

The Twin Towers laughed as one of them took the ball out of bounds and passed it to his brother. They controlled the ball passing it back and forth to one another, Bones watched the twins closely. He spotted the point guard coming up for a pick. He caught it, stepped forward, ran around the pick, stole the ball and raced down the court. He realized he was by himself. He tossed the ball in the air and caught it for a tomahawk slam.

The crowd went into a frenzy. Bones waved his arms up and down to the crowd as he gave his teammate a hi-five. The next five minutes the twins made jump shot after jump shot. Bones was double teamed and forced to make his other teammates play. Chad McLaughlin missed a 17-footer, grabbed the rebound and slammed it in hard. He ran down the court taunting the Braintree bench.

The Braintree coach called a time out. He barked at his players. He pointed to the twins and closed his fist. The next four minutes the twins became unstoppable, as they put on a clinic by bullying their way in the paint and shooting rainbow shots that hit all nets. The clinic they put on made Avon jump to an 11-point lead.

Lynn was starting to get worried as she watched the momentum of the game change. It was starting to look like it could become a blowout. She stood up in her seat and shouted. "BRAINTREE, BRAINTREE, BRAINTREE."

The crowd picked up and started yelling the same thing. Bones heard the chants and looked at the crowd and felt the game was all his. He grabbed the inbound pass and dribbled between a few defenders and pulled up to the three-point line and shot it.

"NETS." Lynn shouted, as she leaned over and kissed Hoop.

Alesia nodded her head and smiled watching the game. She was glad that Bones decided to do something different than murder people. Alesia replaced Lynn as the project's prettiest female. Her Indian roots blossomed in her features. In Bromley-Heath they called her Red-Dot: for red dot Indian.

Bones got back on defense, jumped and blocked one of the twins' jump shots. The ball went to Bones' power forward who passed the ball to the point guard. The point guard raced down the court, spotted Bones and threw a no-look behind the back pass. Bones stopped dribbling, waved Hi to his defender, crossed him over Tim Hardaway style and shot his famous 17-footer.

Avon's point guard launched the ball across to Brad McLaughlin who caught it and dunked it with ease. As he ran down the court, he ran his fingers through his blonde hair.

Bones looked up at the scoreboard and saw there were 23 seconds left in the first half. He grabbed the ball and walked up the court. His team was down by eight points. He made it to half-court and bounced passed the ball to his center, who slammed it in and hung on the rim a little too long. The referee called a technical foul.

One of the twins came up and shot a pair of free throws that made all nets. Bones shook his head and realized the twins were well worth the hype.

The horn squawked and Bones and his teammates walked toward the locker room. As Bones made his way toward the locker room, he saw Dr. Alexander and her daughter standing in the lobby.

"Good half Alfred." Dr. Alexander commented.

Bones looked and saw Dr. Alexander and her daughter. He double looked at her daughter and admired her beauty.

"Alfred, I want to introduce you to my daughter Hollis. Alfred this is Hollis and Hollis this is Alfred."

"My daughter attends Boston College for mental health counseling. Alfred, if you want your team to win then it's up to you, you have to take over the next half. This will be your best chance to win a state title against such a quality team and if you win against those twins then the sky's the limit."

"My mom is right. Take it to the bank and follow up on your misses." Hollis said.

"I'm going to try to give it my all."

"No! You are going to give your all because "try" means to fail. I'm going to let you go join your team and we will see you when you raise that trophy in the air." Dr. Alexander said.

Bones couldn't help but to stare at Hollis. He wanted to say something, but he could only manage to smile. He hugged both of them and walked into the locker room. He joined his teammates and gave them some inspiration for the next half.

Ten minutes later Bones and his teammates walked out the locker room. He stopped as he saw his mother and what looked like his whole housing project on the stairs.

"BONES." He heard someone yell.

Bones walked toward the crowd and hugged and kissed his mother. He looked at how pretty Alesia was and how big her son had become. Hoop stepped forward and reached out his hand. Bones was confused, he always heard of Hoop, but had only seen him a few times in his younger years.

"This is Hoop," His mother said joyously.

"What up," Bones said, as he gave Hoop a hug.

Over Hoop's shoulder Bones spotted Menace hand going across his throat in a cut throat manner. Bones nodded his head, not sure what Menace meant.

"Good half, one more to go." Hoop said as he thought about the 18 & under team he coached.

"Thanks. I'm going to do my best to bring the trophy back to the project in my honor." Bones said confidently.

Bones walked up to his grandmother, hugged and thanked her for coming and showing support. He turned and threw the Boston three finger salute to Menace and joined his teammates on the court.

The next half Bones was doing most of the scoring for his team. The Twin Towers were too much as they made 17-footer after 17-footer. Bones knew his team needed four 3-pointers to get back into the game. He decided to put his team on his shoulders and put on a clinic of his own. He clapped his hand, grabbed the inbound pass, crossed over his defender, stopped at the top of the key and shot a three pointer that was all net. He wiped off the sweat on his forehead, got back on defense, stole the ball and spotted another three pointer and shot it.

The crowd watched as Bones single handedly turned the game around. The next seven minutes Braintree defense put the clamps on the Twin Towers. Bones passed the ball to his center who gave a series of head fakes and went up and under his defender for an easy two off the backboard.

"GET BACK ON DEFENSE." Bones yelled to his team.

The Twin Towers were becoming frustrated and kept looking at the clock. This was the first time in their four years at Avon high that they were on the verge of losing.

"SIX-FIVE-FOUR-THREE-TWO-ONE." The crowd shouted as Bones threw the ball in the air.

Mr. Thibodeau ran onto the court and grabbed Bones. He kissed Bones on his forehead and then hugged him like a father. "We did it. We did it. We won our first championship since the sixties."

Bones walked over and grabbed Menace's Miami Heat hat, tossed it on, grabbed the trophy from the scorer's table and winked at the Twin Towers who were shedding tears. Bones lifted the trophy high in the air and raised his index finger symbolizing #1 His Miami Heat hat covered his eyes as cameras snapped from every angle.

Chapter 30

Bones walked off the court like he had won the NBA championship. Tomorrow he would be the most talked about player in the state, maybe even the country. He smiled at the thought of him holding the trophy with the Miami Heat hat inches from his eyebrows. He walked through the tunnel, took a left and heard his name.

"Alfred."

Bones turned around and spotted his mother and Hoop. He smiled at his mother and stared at Hoop. Bones was a different person these days. He became a man with a mission to take his skills to the next level.

"Good game baby," Lynn said hugging her son.

"I did it for you ma!"

"I know you did."

"That was quite a performance all-star, what fifty points?"

"Nah! It was more like fifty-seven points, sixteen rebounds and 6 steals." Bones bragged.

"Damn! That's what is needed for the Heath Mob eighteen and under squad." Hoop said.

"We have a squad?" Bones asked.

"Yeah! We have a summer team in the BNBL League and we are far from the best."

"What happened to Speedy and Menace? What they don't ball no more?"

"They ball, but the other teams have more explosive players."

"Like who?"

"H-Block!"

"Who the fuck is H-Block?"

"Last summer they took every tournament from the BNBL to the Chill Will league at Washington Park. They are the team to beat in the BNBL since Orchard Park got a lifetime expulsion."

"I'm here for the Heath Mob. Who else do we have on our team besides Menace and Speedy?"

"We have the young nigga Snake. He has some good moves in the paint."

"Snake. Who's that?"

"You know Snake or you might remember him as Jalen Jones. He's Richie Jones' little brother."

"Oh! I know him. They call him Snake now?"

"Yeah! So, how long do you have in this program?"

"I'm phasing out, but in the summer, I will be granted a sixty-day home pass. Hoop you already know where I'll be."

"I no longer go by Hoop; the name is the Commissioner."

Bones looked at Hoop like he had two heads. Bones wasn't calling anyone the Commissioner.

"Yeah, whatever Hoop."

"Like I said, it's the Commissioner, Hoop is a thing of the past. How would you like if I called you Alfred?"

"I would honor that because I'm a reflection of my father in more ways than you think. Speaking of my father ma, when was the last time you heard from him?"

"A couple months back. He said that you two had been in contact through letters."

"Yup! I can't wait till he comes home. I miss my old man." Bones smiled.

"Baby, I can't believe how good you had played out their today. Pretty soon every college in the country is going to want you."

"I hope so cause all the letters I had been getting were from local colleges."

"Believe me, after the performance you put on tonight, they will be contacting you." Lynn said, as she reached in and gave her son a hug. "I know I haven't been writing to you, but you know that your moms always love you." Lynn said as she gave her son a hug.

"Come on ma, I know that and I love you too."

"Alright baby, we have to go." Hoop said wrapping his left arm around Lynn's shoulder. "You played a good game Alfred; I hope you play that good for us in the summer league."

"Don't worry Hoop, I will play my hardest and bring that title back to the P where it belongs." Bones said as he gave his mother a kiss and walked into his locker room.

Bones took a shower and walked out of the T.D. Bank Garden with his coach. They both had their spirits up. Mr. Thibodeau was ecstatic that his team finally won the state title and Bones finally had got the exposure he needed. He walked into the parking lot and over to the team van.

"I did it, I accomplished my goal of being a winner. Now let me repeat this in my quest to conquer this summer league." Bones thought

Chapter 31

Lynn, Alesia and Royce were visiting a friend in the Columbia Point housing project.

"You know English High is playing at UMass. My nephew plays for them." Lynn's friend Classy said.

"I went to English back in the day and the basketball team sucked. Did they get any better?"

"They are really good. They have one of the best players in the city of Boston. He calls himself ESPN." Classy informed.

"I bet he can't touch my son on the court." Lynn said, as she thought about how her son performed the other night at the T.D. Garden. "I want to see this ESPN guy, let's get in this gym and watch this game."

The Commissioner was inside the gym at UMass Boston with a female name "Dollar." They were watching English High play in the Division 4 state finals against a school from the South Shore. Hoop kept his eyes on a six-foot ten center who was called ESPN: for his highlights.

ESPN was H-Blocks best player and one of the best ball players to come out of Roxbury in the past 25 years. His height and his low post moves made him unstoppable. He had footwork similar to the great Hakeem Olajuwon.

During the last two summers Bromley-Heath practically became a non-factor in the inner-city basketball circuit. He hoped Bones was a man of his word and believed that, if Bones were to bring his talent to the Heath Mob, they would be able to give H-Block a run for their money.

ESPN flew down the court like a bat, crossed over his defender and went up for a pump slam. The crowd cheered, as ESPN held onto the rim taunting his defender.

"Do you think he's the best the city ever saw?" Dollar asked.

"Nah! There was a nigga from Mission Hill some years back better than him. Plus no one was ever better than Smooth Simpson from my project." Hoop said looking at Dollar. They finished watching the game, stepped outside of the gym and were stopped dead in their tracks by Lynn and her friends.

Lynn's eyes grew wide as she saw her man with another female. Lynn shook her head side to side and stepped up to Dollar's face.

"Who's this bitch?" Lynn asked, pointing her index finger in Dollars face.

Dollar knocked Lynn's hand out of her face and grabbed her arm and twisted it, curling Lynn's body sideways. Alesia reached into her pocket and grabbed a box razor, clicked out the razor and in one swift motion sliced Dollar in the face.

"ARGH." Dollar screamed, releasing her grip on Lynn's arm.

Dollar grabbed the side of her face as the blood gushed out. She looked at Alesia and then at the Commissioner. Lynn closed her fist and punched Dollar in the face. The force of Lynn's punch knocked her down and the girls pounded Dollar with hands and feet. Hoop stepped a few feet back and watched the action. He intervened by grabbing Lynn off of Dollar and pushing the other girls out of the way.

"ENOUGH." He yelled.

Lynn looked at him with fire in her eyes. She couldn't believe she caught her man red handed with another female. The thought of another female taking her place disgusted her.

"Who is this bitch?" Lynn said, pointing at Dollar.

"My business." Hoop laughed.

"YOU'RE BUSINESS." Lynn shouted.

"Yeah! My business."

"I like that Jose, I like that." Lynn laughed, looking at him in the eyes.

"You're still number one." He said with a smile.

As Dollar got up front he ground, Lynn saw the cut on her face for the first time. She looked at the cut and knew it had to be from the box razor she had given Alesia a few weeks earlier. She smiled and realized that the wounded girl was a thing of the past.

"You can have her. She's damaged goods anyway."

Hoop looked at Dollar and saw the cut on her face. He shook his head, grabbed Dollar and walked away. They walked to his sedan. He popped the trunk, grabbed a towel and pressed it against her face.

"Hold it right until we get to the hospital." Hoop said.

Lynn watched her man pull off in his car. "I'm going back to the P." Lynn said walking toward her Mercedes.

Hoop drove to the hospital and pulled into the emergency exit. He reached in his pocket, pulled out a knot of 100-dollar bills and peeled off two thousand dollars. "That's for food and shelter. I'm sorry, give me a kiss."

Dollar leaned over and gave Hoop a kiss on his soft lips. She smiled and opened the door with the towel still pressed on her face. Hoop watched her walk through the electronic sliding doors and then pulled off.

Lynn was fuming as she drove down Columbus Avenue and hit the right blinker and turned onto Centre Street. Alesia was in the passenger seat and Royce sat in the back. They were quiet, as Lynn yelled every expletive in the book. Lynn whipped her Mercedes into the parking lot. For the next few minutes they sat in the car listening to Lynn cursing. From the backseat Royce saw Hoop's Mercedes pulling beside Lynn.

"There he goes," Royce pointed.

Lynn looked and sucked her teeth. Hoop grabbed his .9mm Kimber from under the seat, tucked it in his waist and opened the door. He stepped out and walked over to the driver's door. He reached and tried to snatch the door open.

"GET OUT OF THE CAR." Hoop shouted.

Lynn looked at him like he had lost his mind. She looked at Royce and Alesia and told them to get out. Hoop stepped back and sat on the hood of his car. Lynn, Royce and Alesia stepped out into the parking lot. Lynn smiled at Hoop.

"You should be ashamed of yourself for trying to play me like I am an average bitch."

Hoop leaped up off the hood and marched over to Lynn. He had anger written all over his face. "Average. You are the average bitch. Don't let all this material shit cloud your vision." Hoop barked, as he stepped in her face.

"Hoop, I'm telling you to get out of my face or else."

"OR ELSE WHAT!" He yelled, grabbing a fist full of her hair and pulled her closer to him.

Menace and Castro were watching from the rooftop of one of the many project seven story buildings. They saw Hoop grab a fist full of Lynn's hair. Menace used his binoculars to look closer at the two.

"You see that?" Menace asked Castro.

"Yeah! That nigga might have signed his death certificate with that one."

"I know."

Alesia and Royce ran up on Hoop and attempted to get him to release the death grip he had on Lynn's hair.

"GET OFF OF HER." Alesia yelled.

"Nah! I'm not going to until she apologizes. I'm a boss and I'll be damned if this average bitch disrespects me and mines."

"I'm sorry baby, I'm sorry baby." Lynn cried.

Hoop released the grip he had on her hair and placed the Kimber back in his waist. He looked at Lynn and told her to come and hug him. Lynn stood there in tears.

Menace fumed as he watched Hoop pull out a gun on his older sister Royce. *"I'm going to get him when he least expects it."* Menace thought.

Lynn walked toward Hoop and hugged him. She cried on his shoulder as her girls watched in shock.

"I'm sorry baby." Hoop whispered in her ear.

"Me too. I love you Jose, I love you." Lynn cried.

Lynn knew for every action there was a reaction and the reaction to her action of whipping the girl outside the gym was him damn near blowing her brains out. Lynn was just glad that no one was out in the project to see what had just unfolded.

Chapter 32

Dr. Alexander got together with Bones' mother and other members of his family and threw a championship party for him at an Italian restaurant on the Fan Pier in Boston called Strega. This was the first time Bones had ever eaten at a five-star restaurant. He enjoyed his time there and during the whole afternoon Dr. Alexander couldn't help but notice how Bones kept staring at her daughter.

"He must like her." Dr. Alexander thought, as she walked over toward her daughter. "Hollis, you should get to know Alfred a little better."

Hollis listened to her mother and walked over toward Bones. She tapped him on his shoulder and he turned around. He was happy to see it was Hollis. The whole afternoon he couldn't help but stare at how flawless her features were.

"Have you ever thought about prep school?" Hollis asked.

"Not really, although a few prep schools contacted me."

"Like who?"

"Notre Dame Prep, Winchendon and M.C.I. in Pittsfield, Maine."

"Thayer Academy never contacted you?"

"Not yet."

"If you want, my mom probably could get you in there for she is good friends with the Dean."

"Nah! I'm straight."

"It would be for your benefit."

"Let me give it some thought."

"Okay. How long were you in the Department of Youth Services for?"

"Since I was thirteen."

"Wow. That is a long time. Do you think that you are rehabilitated?"

"Of course. I will never be back in that place. I love basketball too much and I believe if I keep at it the way I am then that will be my future."

"I know all so well about playing basketball. I play for Boston College, even though we aren't that good, just the feeling of stepping onto the floor at the Conde Arena makes my adrenaline pump like crazy."

"I never knew you played ball."

"Yeah, many people don't." Hollis giggled, "Where are you going from here?"

"To my mother's place."

"If you need a ride then I will take you there."

"Okay."

Twenty minutes later they wrapped it up at Strega's and Bones left with Hollis. They continued a deep conversation about personal development as they drove toward Bromley-Heath Project. As they neared the project Hollis felt a chill when she spotted all the project kids, gangsters and hustlers on Centre Street and outside of Jackson Square.

"Are you sure you want to be around this area?" Hollis asked as she reflected back to all the news coverage that this project had in the past couple years.

"This is home base." Bones said.

"Just be safe out here." Hollis said parking in front of a project building.

Bones opened the door, grabbed his bags from the rear seat and looked at the high-rise buildings of his project and wondered if his crew were still called the Rooftop Boys. He turned around and leaned inside of the car and gave Hollis a kiss on the cheek.

"Thanks, and when I get a phone, I will get your number from your moms."

"That will do." Hollis said, as she put the car in drive and pulled off.

From the rooftop Menace was the first one to spot Bones. He smiled at Castro and said. "Cuzzo's back."

"What!" Castro said, grabbing his binoculars. "YES SIR! HE IS." He shouted.

Bones walked past scores of project kids with Miami Heat hats and shirts on. He had yet to recognize a face he remembered.

"Ohh, Wooh!" Menace gave the hood call.

Bones turned around and spotted his best friend with his cousin Castro on the project stairs. He walked over toward them smiling like a Cheshire cat.

"Welcome back my nigga," Menace said, as he grabbed his man for a hug.

"Where is everybody at?"

"This shit is crazy out here, the nigga Juicy."

"What?" Bones said. He was shocked that his crew had a dead homie.

"Yeah! That's why we created this saying in the project: to remember Juicy and others."

"What is it?" Bones asked.

"On dawgs."

"What does that mean?"

"It means rest in peace to all the dead homies in the P."

"When a nigga say 'on dawgs' that means a nigga is telling the truth and, if a nigga lies on it, then it's an automatic beat down and expulsion from the project." Castro said.

"That's deep."

"Let's go over to the benches and see what is good with punk ass Speedy. That sucker ass nigga was the getaway driver when Juicy got killed. I'm doing my research and, when it's done, a conclusion is going to be swift and furious." Menace snarled.

Alesia looked out of her window and saw Bones walk toward the benches with Menace and Castro. Her eyes watered every time she saw the little terror. She knew every time he stepped foot in the project something bad happened.

"Mommy, who's that?"

"That's Alfred, but everyone calls him Bones, he's violent. Stay away from him." Alesia said walking away from the window.

Bones, Menace and Castro joined Speedy, Skitzo and a young gang-ster named Snake on the benches. Speedy had some dark shades on his face to shield the two black eyes that Menace and Castro gave him for leaving Juicy to die in the street.

"Alfy what's up dawg?" Skitzo said, getting off the benches.

"Yo! What's up?"

"Last time I saw you, it was a lot of rat-tat-tat going off." Skitzo smiled.

"That was then," Bones said looking at Speedy. "When is Juicy's fu-neral?"

"Friday."

Menace walked over and stood directly in front of Speedy. He burnt holes through Speedy with his eyes. Speedy looked up, saw Menace and lowered his head like he was a kid on punishment.

"We got a game Saturday down at Trotter Park," Menace said.

"Against who?" Bones asked.

"H-Block."

"I heard a lot about this ESPN cat. Is he good as advertised?" Bones asked.

"To be real dawg, the nigga is the truth and hard to stop in the paint because of his height and his long ass arms." Menace said.

"I can't wait to put the brakes on his ass. I just destroyed the Twin Towers and they both were his height." Bones laughed.

"It ain't easy as you think dawg. That nigga has a seven foot three wing span and moves like a guard." Menace said.

Loud music caught their attention. They turned toward Centre Street and saw a pretty sky-blue Maserati Quattroporte sitting on gold Asante rims. Bones looked at the car and wondered who was behind the wheel.

"That's the commissioner." Bones heard Snake said.

Bones looked at Hoop parking his car. Menace walked over to Bones and pulled him to the side.

"You know that nigga is fucking your mother. A few weeks back he was being disrespectful pointing guns at her and pulling her hair in the project."

"WHAT!" Bones shouted, "Nigga don't play with me. Are you telling me that he had violated my mom's?"

"Yeah! He violated her. I know you want to get at that nigga for that sucker shit, but be easy let's rock him to sleep cause these days he's not too easy to get with. All his cars are bullet-proof. He's out here winning dawg. I have never seen no one like this."

Hoop stepped out of the Maserati one ostrich sandal at a time. Bones looked closely at the nigga who took his uncle Greenback's place as project boss. Hoop stood up and wiped off the wrinkles in his linen and walked toward the crew. Bones saw that Hoop's linen short set matched the exterior of his car and the ostrich sandals matched the interior.

Hoop reached them and gave dap to each member of the Heath Mob. He stopped at Bones and reached out his hand. "Welcome back. I have a bag of money for you little homie."

"Thanks," Bones said as he shook Hoop's hand.

"We're ready when you're ready big homie." Skitzo said.

Hoop nodded and walked away. Bones looked at the tri-color diamond bracelet and knew that it was top quality diamonds. Hoop stopped, turned and said, "Bones, we have a game Saturday against H-Block and your talent is needed."

"It feels like we are under dictatorship. We can't do shit on our own." Castro complained.

Menace knew Hoop was on some bullshit. He wasn't feeling him too much these days and just like the others who felt they were bigger than the world, all it took was a bullet to the head and they would just be memories. He looked at Bones and smiled because he knew that, with Bones back in the fold, nothing could stop them.

* * * * * *

Alesia sat on the stairs by her side was a drawstring bag with over thirty thousand dollars in small bills. She used her business skills to conduct her weed operation. She had two of the prettiest young girls in the project hustling for her.

Nyami and Myami were the nieces of Lynn and the daughters of Greenback. When they came of age, they decided to hustle weed. Alesia set them up with their own apartment and a building to use as a distribution center. The twins had all the younger generation copping from them.

Alesia's business mind came from studying and watching family members and listening to the jewels her baby father once dropped. All her studious ways paid off. She was able to create gimmicks, calculate her gross margin and monitor her cash flow. During the morning hours she enrolled in a business management class at Bunker Hill Community College. In the afternoon she worked as Mrs. Mary's secretary. The classes began paying off. She became an A student and was ready to take the next step into opening up a few business ventures with the support of a few committed investors. Alesia saw Hoop's diamond bracelet shining brightly as he walked through the project. She stood up so he could see her. He spotted her and made his way toward her.

"There goes the Commissioner," her son pointed.

Alesia walked up, hugged and passed him the bag. Hoop reached in his pocket and passed her son a fifty-dollar bill. The other kids saw Hoop pass Tragdon the money and ran up to him. He passed each kid a fifty-dollar bill.

"Save every dollar that is given to you," Alesia whispered in her son's ear.

Tragdon just nodded his head and stuffed the money in the pocket of his tiny guess jeans. He has been saving all the money that Hoop and other hustlers in the project had been giving him. He was at the age where he wanted to know who had murdered his father. Alesia kept secret who was the ones responsible and every time he asked, she told him that she didn't know.

Chapter 33

On the day of Juicy's funeral it was pouring rain. The streets were soaked with puddles of water. The funeral was held at Greater Love Tabernacle Church in Dorchester, Massachusetts. The service was paid in full by Hoop. He supplied dozens of flowers that decorated the church and casket. He bought a half of a dozen burial lots with tomb-stones in advance. He wanted all his niggas to be buried in the same area that he called "Heath Way." He even had a custom-made street sign for those who didn't know their way around the cemetery. Juicy's solid gold casket was closed as a result of the .44 slug having destroyed his face.

Bones helped carry the casket, as he and other Heath Mob members were the pallbearers. He decided to get Juicy's name tattooed on the back of his left hand. Hoop stood across the street, eyeing the service under a Gucci umbrella. He stood as each Heath Mob member stepped out of the church. He saw Bones and called him.

Bones heard Hoop call him over. He crossed the street and stood next to him. He looked down at Hoop's footwear and noticed his suede Gucci sneakers. *"What type of nigga wear suede in the rain."*

"We have that game against H-Block tomorrow and anything less than a win is unacceptable." Hoop said.

"We're going to win."

"I hope so," Hoop said, as he bent down and picked up the same drawstring bag that Alesia gave him days earlier. "That's thirty stacks. Welcome home all-star."

Bones clutched the bag, looked at Hoop and assured him that a win was indeed necessary.

Chapter 34

H-Block was an area in Roxbury that comprised five streets: Holworthy, Harrishoff, Harold, Homestead and Humboldt. All were in close proximity to Trotter Park.

Trotter Park was a playground and basketball court directly behind the William Monroe Trotter Elementary School on Humboldt Avenue. A group of neighborhood kids called Trotter Park their home base and adopted the Houston Astros baseball caps. This group of kids came from all of the streets in the area that began with the letter H. Hence, the name "H-Block."

ESPN was catching alley-oops when the Bromley-Heath van pulled up to the park. Scattered around the school yard and park were over two dozen H-Block members.

"That's ESPN," Speedy pointed at the tall lanky ball player.

Bones watched as ESPN caught alley-oops with ease. Bones laughed loudly and opened the sliding door and stepped out. The rest of the Heath Mob followed Bones' lead as he marched to the basketball court with a smirk on his face. He noticed they were greeted with ice grills and stares. Bones saw a female with shoulder length dreads, army fatigues and a black T-shirt had the meanest stare of them all.

Menace passed Bones the ball. He dribbled and tossed the ball to the backboard, caught it with his left hand and slammed it in. He grabbed the ball and set up for a 17-footer, shot it and watched as it hit the bottom of the net. Menace smiled at what Bones brought to the game. He knew it was going to be competitive.

Bones stepped to the center of the court. The referee came forward with the ball and tossed it in the air. ESPN out jumped Bones and tapped it to his point guard. ESPN raced down the court and clapped his hands. The point guard passed the ball to ESPN. He grabbed it, backed down Snake up and laid it in with ease.

"GET USE TO IT, IT'S ALL DAY." ESPN taunted.

Menace took the ball out of bounds and passed it to Bones. Bones dribbled up the court and left behind a trail of defenders holding their ankles in awe of his ball handling skills. He shot a behind the back pass to Speedy who tossed it to Snake in the paint. Snake gave a head fake, saw Bones coming from his left and passed it. Bones grabbed it and shot it from the baseline.

"NETS." He yelled.

ESPN smirked at the revamped Bromley-Heath Team. He took the ball out of bounds and was stripped by Menace who bounced passed it to Bones who jumped up and dunked the ball hard rattling the rim.

"HEATH STREET." Menace yelled running down the court.

The female with the dreads inched closer to the court. Bones watched her closely and knew that in her pocket was a gun.

H-Block's point guard dribbled the ball up the court and left Bones holding his ankles. He stopped and laughed at him, then stutter stepped and passed the ball to ESPN who went in for a two-handed slam.

"I TOLD YOU TO GET USE TO IT." ESPN bragged pointing to Bones.

Bones loved competition. He had never before played against a really competitive team. Menace passed the ball to Bones who dribbled up the court and passed it to Snake. ESPN came up, stripped the ball and raced down the court by himself.

"HERE IT COMES," One of H-Block members at courtside yelled.

The whole Heath Mob team watched as ESPN jumped in the air and finished with a Vince Carter Tomahawk dunk.

"Damn!" Menace said, holding his hand over his mouth.

ESPN ran down the court pointing to Bones smiling. Bones shook his head and took the ball out of bounds. Menace controlled the ball as he floated up the court and saw Bones on the opposite side. He stopped his dribble and pointed for his defender to step up. The defender waved his hands and reached for the ball.

"*Mistake, mistake.*" Menace thought, as he crossed over, making his defender fall to one knee. That's what Menace wanted to see, a defender with weak knees. He dribbled in the paint and watched the two defenders come to guard him. He made a behind the back pass to Bones who cut in, grabbed it and gave the crowd a highlight of his own, as he double pumped it for a slam.

"Now that is what you call teamwork." Menace said, as he gave Bones a hi-five.

The Heath Mob hooted and hollered. Bones smiled like he was Michael Jordan hunching his shoulders. He didn't notice ESPN waiting at the other end of the court until it was too late. The only thing he saw was a half court pass that was caught by ESPN who dunked it and hung on the rim. As he came down Menace cocked his fist back and swung it forward.

"CRACK." He broke ESPN's jaw.

H-Block watched their star player fall to the ground unconscious. They flooded the court. Menace threw a few punches on the ones who ran in his direction. Bones kept his eyes on the female as she pulled out a chrome handgun out of her pocket.

"I knew it," Bones said, as he shouted "HIT THE GROUND. HIT THE GROUND," as he got low to the ground.

"POP, POP, POP," The female aimed at any Heath Mob member she saw.

The Heath Mob ran toward the van. Bones was the last one to make it to the van.

"POP, POP." The female squeezed off two shots before running into an alley.

The female who busted shots at the Heath Mob was called Hitler. She came out of the alley and watched as the van came toward her. She raised the gun and squeezed the trigger.

Bones saw Hitler step out of the alley with a gun raised. "SWITCH LANES, SWITCH LANES." He shouted. The driver was too late as three shots rang out.

POP, POP, POP." Hitler emptied the last three shots out her .25 handgun.

The Bromley-Heath van swerved and side swiped three parked cars. The driver took a right down Townsend Street and made his escape.

Hitler ran out of the alley and passed the .25 to an H-Block member named Bragging Brad. A stolen Honda Civic pulled up and Hitler hopped in. Alley-Cat was driving the stolen car while Predator was in the passenger seat. Hitler sat back and pulled her dreads into a ponytail. Predator passed her a .380 Taurus. They made it to Jamaica Plain in no time. Hitler directed traffic and told Alley-Cat to pull across the street from Bromley-Heath Street Project and let her out.

What many didn't know was that ten years back it was rumored that members of the Heath Street Gang had murdered her father. She always held hatred for anyone in that project ever since.

Alley-Cat pulled to a side street across from the project and let Hitler out. She walked over and sat on the bumper of an abandoned car and waited for any sign of a Heath Street member.

* * * * * *

Bones' mind was racing, as he thought about how close he was to getting shot and Hollis's words. *"Be safe around here."* He looked at Menace who had a smirk on his face and wondered what was going through his best friend's mind.

"I knew I should have brought the gun." Menace growled.

Hitler saw the van coming up Centre Street and stepped from her hiding spot and raised the Taurus.

"BOC, BOC, BOC, BOC, BOC."

The van screeched and ran head first into a parked car. Predator came from where he was hiding, ran up to the van, snatched open the door, aimed the .9mm Hi-Point and pulled the trigger. "BOC, BOC, BOC, BOC, CLICK, CLICK, CLICK, CLICK." The gun jammed. Predator turned the gun upside down and beamed it at Menace's head. The handle of the gun clocked him in the dome. Menace grabbed his head.

"I'M HIT. I'M HIT." Bones yelled, as he felt his left leg go numb. Snake and Speedy grabbed him out of the van and carried him over to the benches.

Three out of the four shots hit Bones in his left leg. He knew at that moment his basketball career was over and that it was on with him and H-Block. He wasn't letting up until he put a few members of the H-Block Gang in the dirt.

Chapter 35

After a few days in Boston Medical Center Bones was transferred to Mass General Hospital to start the procedure to amputate his left leg. The bullets that smashed his leg were Black Rhinos.

The Black Rhino bullet is made of carbon-based plastics called polymers instead of metal, a substance that will pierce through bullet-proof vests. What makes the bullet lethal is that it breaks apart once it hits flesh with a razor type wire.

Bones couldn't believe his luck. He was hit with some of the most powerful bullets on earth. He knew that once he got his prosthetic leg and was back on the streets, he was going to go full steam ahead at destroying H-Block.

The doctor stood at his bedside giving him a lecture on how those who had their legs amputated had overcome major obstacles. Bones blanked out the doctor's words and focused on his own thoughts.

"One leg Alfy-B," Bones thought.

"Yeah! That would do." Bones smiled.

The doctor finished his speech and left the room. Bones hated him. Since his arrival the doctor has been the bearer of bad news.

Ten minutes after the doctor had left the room the door opened and Hollis and Dr. Alexander walked in with a dozen red roses in a black vase.

"*Miami Heat colors.*" Bones looked at the two and became sad that they had to see him in such a vulnerable position. He watched as they placed the vase on the end table and sat in plastic chairs.

"How are you feeling Alfred?" Dr. Alexander asked.

"Under these circumstances, I guess I am feeling good. It's a tough thing to go through physically and mentally knowing that my left leg would be amputated."

"I'm not disappointed, angry or mad at you for being here. We all make decisions and some are good and some are bad. We do not know which ones are bad until something happens. I knew this was a bad decision to go back there because when I dropped you off the area just looked like trouble." Hollis said.

"I spoke to the doctor and he told me about the procedure you will be going through to get your leg amputated and upon hearing that I shedded tears. The thought of them removing tissue and any crushed bone sounds so painful and for it to be you to go through this is terrible." Dr. Alexander said.

"I know, it's hard to think about what is going to happen to me next." Bones said, "All I have to do is let GOD be the judge of me and my life from this point forward."

"So, once everything boils over what is your backup plan now that your basketball career is over?" Hollis asked.

"I don't know. I haven't even thought that far ahead to be honest."

"You have a few things going for you and one of those is that you have no adult criminal record. Once you finish your last year of high school, I could help you get enrolled in the University of New Hampshire." Dr. Alexander said.

"New Hampshire." Bones mumbled.

"Yes! New Hampshire. It would put you on the right track and away from these streets who haven't been any good to you. I would help you get into the medical field.

Bones knew that would require at least another ten years of schooling and he wasn't ready to pursue a dream in the medical field. He just wanted retaliation for what had happened to him and how his basketball career ended.

"You need to think about what you want in life and how you are going to pursue it. My daughter is heartbroken about what happened to you and if you know what I know that girl likes you."

Bones looked over at Hollis and saw tears welling up in her eyes. He said a few words and both mother and daughter gave him a kiss and walked out. The next hour he sat in his bed watching gangland on Spike T.V. He heard the door open and looked to see who was entering and was happy to see his mother walk in with Hoop.

"Hey ma." Bones said, as he sat upright in his bed.

"Hey baby, how are you feeling?" Lynn said, as she started to cry.

"I'm feeling a little pain, but other than that I'm feeling good. I spoke to the doctor and learned that they would have to remove the diseased tissue and any crushed bone. Then smooth uneven areas of bone and seal off blood vessels and nerves, cut and shape my muscles so that the stump will be able to have an artificial limb (prosthesis) attached to it. What doesn't kill me only will make me stronger. But I know once I get better, I'm not going to be a nice guy especially to those who have done this to me. I don't deserve all that I'm going through. I was just there to play ball; a fight broke out and I'm the only one to get shot. That is bullshit." Bones said looking at Hoop.

"Haste is not necessary. We have to use our minds and attack when they least expect."

"Fuck them. I'm not going out like no sucker. Look at my leg." Bones said pointing to the bandages that covered his leg. "I'm the one who is going to be walking around with a fake leg."

"Like I said, revenge is necessary, but let's not be hasty. In this project my words are law." Hoop said.

Bones chuckled to himself, looked at Hoop and shook his head. "Whatever, nigga. I'm going to make them suckers feel the pressure of my heat. If it was you who got shot, then you would call the wolves and you know it."

"How long will this surgery take?" Hoop asked.

"Between two to three hours."

Lynn stood over her son crying. She knew from the conversation between him and Hoop that their words would one day turn into a conflict and that she did not want to witness.

While Bones was laying up in Mass General hospital his best friend

Menace was honoring him with extreme violence. He put his beef with all the gangs his project were at war with and took out his anger on H-Block.

Bragging Brad, Hitler and Predator sat in a Jeep Cherokee on Harold Street.

"I'm about to go to the Worthy to see if there's any paper up there," Bragging Brad said, getting out of the Jeep.

"Alright! We are going to see you in a few hours. It's time to take a nap." Predator said.

Menace watched Bragging Brad spin the corner on Holworthy Street. The Houston Astros hat gave him away. "It's hammer time." Menace mumbled.

Bragging Brad was one of H-Block's most feared gangsters. He had an itchy trigger finger. The dozens of shootings he had done citywide gave him his name, as he explained to anyone who was willing to listen. He took a liking to bragging about his gung-ho exploits.

Bragging Brad saw a fiend cross the street. "Oohh, Wooh!" He gave the hood call.

The fiend stopped, turned around and saw him. They met in the middle of the street, right in front of an alley. Inside the alley was Menace. He stepped to the mouth of the alley, raised the .357 automatic and pulled the trigger.

"BOOM, BOOM, BOOM BOOM."

Two of the four bullets crashed into Bragging Brad's back paralyzing him immediately. The fiend he was serving, bent down, reached in Brad's pocket, grabbed the money and ran down the street with a few twenties of crack and money to cop more. Menace reached in his pocket, grabbed the ski mask and wrapped it on his face. He walked out the alley and over to where Bragging Brad laid in the street. He placed the gun to his face and pulled the trigger three times.

"THAT'S HOW YOU KILL A MAN." Menace shouted, as he ran away toward his getaway car.

Chapter 36

The tail of a candy apple green Cadillac Escalade was wide open. Spanish Dan, Lazy and Skitzo were passing out black minks to all the Heath Mob members and red minks to the Femme Fatales. He did this every year to show that he gave back to the community. After all, it was October 1st the official start of mink season, a day that Hoop had coined Hustler's Appreciation Day.

While the whole project was celebrating Hustler's Appreciation Day, Bones was being discharged from Mass General hospital. The hospital gave him crutches to help him walk. He saw on T.V. a replacement to crutches called the iWALK 2.0 and he told his mother about it and she ordered it. The iWALK 2.0 Hands-Free Knee Crutch is a crutch that ends the pain and inconvenience of conventional crutches. By Bones using the iWALK 2.0 he would be allowed to lead a functional, hands-free, pain-free life during his rehabilitation or until his prosthetic leg was delivered.

Lynn helped her son get in the passenger seat of her Mercedes Benz. Bones reclined the seat and looked out of the window as his mother navigated through the city. They stopped at a red light on Columbus Avenue. Bones looked at the buildings that made up the Dark Side outside of Academy Market stood close to a gang-members wearing Atlanta Braves caps, sweaters and jackets.

"I hope you have a clear mind son, and keep praying to GOD because he is the reason why you are still alive."

"Of course, I have a clear mind and I am happy to be alive. Those bullets I got hit with were designed to kill people. Home sweet home." Bones said, rubbing his hands together.

Lynn pulled into the parking lot and saw a crowd at the Escalade. She popped the trunk and grabbed his iWALK 2.0 and helped her son get out of the Mercedes. She helped him ease into it and together they walked over to where members of the Heath Mob were passing out mink coats.

While Bones was in the hospital Hoop had addressed all of the drama that was sure to come from the murder of Bragging Brad by initiating a peace treaty between his project and H-Block. He had talks with a few of H-Block's elders and pointed the finger to Orchard Park. One thing Hoop wasn't going to do was bring unnecessary heat to his project. The money he made city wide showed him that it was M.O.E. (Money Over Everything).

Bones used the iWalk 2.0 to maneuver to where his cousin Lazy was passing out mink coats. Bones saw Alesia and a few other females from the project wearing red mink coats.

"What's up cuz?" Bones said, as he reached his cousin Lazy.

Lazy paused, looked at Bones and his eyes started to water. He walked over toward him and gave him a tight hug. He hugged him so tight that Bones almost lost his breath.

"I'm glad that you are back, little cuz. Just hearing about what happened to you brought out the worst in me and others in this project. Let me give you a mink in courtesy of the "The Commissioner." He grabbed a coat and walked behind Bones and placed it on him. "I love you and get better."

"I will. I'm just waiting for my prosthetic and then I will be back out here with niggas." Bones said.

* * * * * *

Menace was watching from the roof top when he saw Lazy place the mink on Bones. Menace declined his fur and anything else that Hoop was giving to the project. He had to show resistance to make Hoop know that all was not under his command.

"ALFY-B," Menace yelled, as he saw Bones walking with his mother using his iWALK 2.0.

Bones looked up and saw his man Menace walking toward him with a butt of a gun sticking out of his waist.

"What's good?" Menace said reaching Bones. "Hey Ms. Barton."

"How are you doing Marco?"

"Good. Good as I can be treated out here in this project."

"I hear that."

"I'm going to let y'all talk and I will be back in a few minutes to take you home Alfred."

"Ok ma."

Menace waited until Lynn disappeared before he started to talk. He looked Bones in his eyes and stated. "I'm fed up with your mother's boyfriend."

"What he do now dawg?"

"The ultimate. He squashed the beef with H-Block and told them that Orchard Park was behind the murder of Bragging Brad."

"Who the fuck is Bragging Brad?"

"One of the top shooters from H-Block."

"That's some sucker shit."

"I'm going to fill you in on this later on. I'm glad to see you back home. It's a lot of catching up we have to do, but first get healthy and I will be out here holding it down." Menace said, as he gave Bones the three-finger handshake before walking away.

Bones used the iWALK 2.0 to walk to where he saw his mother standing. He walked over to her and greeted her friends and together they walked to their apartment building on Heath Street. In the back of Bones mind he couldn't believe that Hoop would squash beef with the crew responsible for his current situation.

Chapter 37

It took some time for Bones to get used to walking with his pros-thetic leg. Every day he and his mother walked from Jackson Square to Ruggles station and back. Since he has been out of the hospital, he has been hearing a lot of things about Hoop that he didn't wasn't fond of.

In a chilly November afternoon Bones walked past the mural of his uncle sitting on a Mercedes Benz station wagon. He read the names on the wall: Randy, Tony Woods, C.Y.G., Loom, Nate Lackland, Mike Seals, Scarface, Troy Smith, Dame Dollar, Bug, T.P, Pete, Jaws, Slick and many others.

"I miss all those niggas." Bones said.

"We do too." Castro said, as him and Menace walked up behind Bones. "What's up Cuddy?"

Bones turned around and saw his cousin Castro and his best friend Menace. He gave both a hug and the three-finger handshake.

"We are about to head to Orchard Park. You are welcome to come. We are about to expose your mother's bitch ass boyfriend." Menace said.

"I will roll with y'all."

They walked over to a black Honda Accord. Bones took the front seat while Menace took the driver seat and Castro took the back seat. Bones noticed that he was the only one without a Miami Heat hat. They pulled up to the Orchard Park housing project in no time. Menace drove down Zeigler Street and parked.

Outside of one of the project buildings stood about six Orchard Park gang members and amongst them were Itchy and Davey-D. Itchy saw the car pull up and walked over toward it.

"Heath Mob, what's good with you." Itchy said as he gave the three-finger handshake to all three members of the Heath Mob.

"We came down here to put you on to some foul shit, you know there is a reason for everything."

"True." Itchy said, raising an eyebrow.

"There's a snake in our garden and if we don't kill him then we all will be poisoned. When I say poisoned, I mean our bond."

"A snake? Who's the snake?"

"Hoop." Menace answered.

"No way, Hoop is a good nigga. He treats everyone fair. You must be joking." Itchy said seriously.

"Nah! The beef with H-Block is originally our beef. It began the day my nigga right here got shot and since then the nigga Hoop been acting like he wants to control our movements on how we attack. Every time niggas bombed on them, they came right back and returned the favor, and for Hoop, that was bad publicity. He wants the project under the radar so the Feds won't snoop. We all know that murders bring the Feds. He reached out to a few elders from H-Block that he met in prison and pointed the finger at your project. He put your niggas in harm's way, all with the intentions of keeping Bromley-Heath off the police radar. We are here to let you know that the Heath Mob can handle our own business."

"Are you sure?" Itchy said, scratching his bald head.

"I'm a man of my word. I would never come down to lie to you or have you gone against one of our own. I just wanted you to know what is going on and how snake like that nigga is. I know you deal with him on the get money tip and all, but it's up to you to make your own deci-sion."

"Damn, Hoop betrayed us for his own safe keeping. Say on dawgs, he betrayed Orchard Park."

"ON DAWGS." Bones, Menace and Castro shouted in unison.

"Nuff said. I will talk to my niggas and see what they want to do about this. So, this is Bones huh. I heard a lot of good things about you from my little nigga Monster. You know he's home."

"He is? Where's he at?"

"Over on the Park side. Go over and check him out. He would be happy to see you."

"I haven't seen that nigga in years. I will def. go and see what's up with my nigga." Bones said with excitement in his voice. He gave dap to him and all the Orchard Park members. Then Menace and Castro walked over to the Park Side of the project.

* * * * * *

Monster, Boyawanda and Quick Nick were sitting on the bleachers watching two of the project's best ball players going one on one for cash. Quick Nick was the first to spot the Heath Mob. He tapped Monster and pointed.

Monster turned and saw the Heath Mob. A smile emerged on his face when he saw Bones' face. He stood up, flung his arms in the air and shouted. "MY NIGGA BONES."

Bones walked up to Monster and gave him a hug. They hugged for what seemed like fifteen minutes. "Damn, dawg last time I saw you we were kids."

"I know. You were on your way to that nut house."

"Yeah, a lot has happened since."

"I heard you was on some NBA shit in D.Y.S. and then you came home and got shot. I was pissed to hear that you got hit up the way you did and then next thing you know them Block kids started to come down here and shoot at us."

"I know. That's why we came down here to put niggas on to what is really going on and how this soft ass nigga Hoop from my bricks sent a message to the elders of H-Block that O.P. was responsible for the murder of Bragging Brad." Bones said, looking Monster in his eyes.

"Word! Hoop did some grimy shit like that. What he thought no one was going to find out?"

"I don't know what he thought." Menace interjected, "but I know we're going to make him pay for this snake shit. Once we get back to the project it's going to be a power shift and if the nigga Hoop want to go to war then he will get bucked down." Menace said seriously.

"If you need me. You know where to find me." Monster said.

"We got this." Castro said.

"Cool." Monster said, as he gave each member of the Heath Mob dap. He watched as they walked away and turned to his crew. "You heard what them niggas just said about that nigga Hoop? If it's what they said is true, I have no problem offing him myself."

"Naw, we got this dawg." Bones said, as he dapped Monster up and him and his crew walked toward where the car was parked at.

Menace drove back to the project and parked on Heath Street. They all stepped out and walked inside the project. Menace passed Bones his ski-hat that had the holes poked in where the eyes supposed to be at.

"What you want me to do with this." Bones said holding the ski-hat in his hand.

"It's yours, do whatever you want with it, but do the right thing." Menace said, as he walked inside of a project building.

Bones placed the ski-hat in his back pocket and walked with his cousin toward where a few older heads were free-styling. He listened as Crillz and Press rhymed old school project classics.

"What's up Alfy," Crillz said, staring at Bones in his eyes.

"Nothing much big homey. What's good with you?"

"Nothing too much just rapping some of these old school classics I wrote back in the nineties."

"I hear that. Good music never goes outdated." Bones said as he gave each of the three master rhymers dap.

"I was rooting for you to bring the project with you to the NBA, but then that fuck shit happened. I'm the first to say I wasn't feeling how that shit went down, but who am I to say what went wrong. I'm glad to see you alive."

"I have to get going and see what's up with my grandma." Bones said as he saw Crown and Thurst walk over. "What's up my gees," Bones said as he gave them dap. He turned around and saw the nigga

Hoop staring at him from some project stairs.

Hoop was standing on the stairs of his old building with a white full-length mink coat. He spotted Bones and Castro. This was his first-time seeing Bones out and about in the project since the shooting. *"Damn, them Black Rhinos tore that nigga leg up."* Hoop said to himself as he studied the way Bones walked.

Bones made it over toward Hoop and they locked eyes without saying a word. It was Hoop who broke the ice.

"What's up Stro, what's up Bones?" Hoop greeted.

"What's up dawg?" Castro said.

Instead of greeting Hoop, Bones turned his head and kept walking past him. Hoop saw that Bones dropped his hat on the ground and picked it up. He noticed the ski hat had holes in the eyes and mouth. "BONES YOU DROPPED YOUR HAT?"

Bones patted his back pocket, turned around and saw Hoop holding the ski-hat. Bones walked over toward him and grabbed his hat out of Hoop's hands. He and Castro walked to the other side of the project. They walked past a set of project benches where the project slut La-La sat.

"Heyyy." La-La said, waving to Bones.

"Hold on cuz, let me have a few words with this bitch La-La." Bones said, as he walked over toward the benches where she sat at. "What 's up girl, take a walk with me." Bones said, as he limped to a hallway on Centre Street.

Hoop stood a few feet away on a set of stairs and watched La-La and Bones enter the hallway. He followed them and silently opened the hallway door just as La-La was getting on her knees. He watched her give Bones felatio while his eyes were closed. "That's right girl, give him some of that super head." Hoop giggled.

Bones opened his eyes and flinched as he saw Hoop standing there with his arms behind his back.

"You get to test the pussy yet. It's good. A little too loose for her age, but it's wet and good. It reminds me of all the pregnant females I fucked in the project. There's only two females in the project I never fucked. Red-Dot and that ugly bitch Malika. The latter was because I just can't fuck anyone ugly as her. Finish your B.I. dawg and don't forget to check that pussy and be the judge yourself. I'll be around the P."

Bones looked at him with fire in his eyes. Hoop's appearance alone made him cringe. He looked down at La-La and shouted. "FINISH BITCH."

La-La finished and Bones pulled his pants up and walked out of the hallway. Hoop was in the alley watching Bones walk out of the hallway. He waited for him near the alley and then he stepped out. His appearance scared Bones who jumped back a few feet.

"Damn! Froggy, another jump like that and you would be in the street," Hoop laughed. "You saw a ghost huh Alfred."

Bones ignored Hoop and walked past him as if he never existed.

"DON'T MAKE THIS PROJECT YOUR GRAVE YARD." Hoop yelled.

"WHAT?" Bones turned around.

"YOU HEARD ME. DON'T MAKE THIS PROJECT BE YOUR GRAVE YARD. CAN'T WIN A WAR WITH NO MONEY AND IN THIS PROJECT I'M THE ONE WITH ALL THE MONEY." Hoop laughed.

Hoop walked backwards out of the project and across the street into a Dominican restaurant. Bones walked to the other side of the project and saw Menace with a few younger heads. Menace saw the look in Bones' eyes and knew something was wrong. He excused himself and walked up to his best friend.

"I need a gun," Bones blurted out.

Menace pulled up his shirt to reveal two .357 handguns. Bones reached in Menace's waist and grabbed one of the guns. He placed it in his waist and looked his best friend in his eye and said.

"This nigga Hoop got to go. He threatened me saying 'Don't let the project be my graveyard.' He must think I'm a bitch because of my disability." Bones said, as he turned around and started marching to the other side of the project.

Menace followed him through the project. Alesia, Royce and Mercedes were standing outside of Bromley Hall with red mink coats. Bones and Menace marched past them.

"Where are y'all stomping to?" Mercedes asked.

"To the New Side of the P." Menace answered.

As they made it to the New Side, Bones saw La-La talking to a female name Taffy near the benches and stopped. "Where is Hoop?"

La-La pointed to the Dominican restaurant. Bones and Menace crossed the street.

Hoop was in the restaurant ordering his favorite dish: Octopus, yellow rice and peas. He had a level three Kevlar vest and twin .40 Glocks in shoulder holsters under his mink coat.

"For here or to go?" A stringy haired Dominican female asked.

"To go," Hoop answered, as he flirted with the owner's daughter. He reached in his pocket, pulled out a knot of 100-dollar bills and passed her one bill. He smiled at her and grabbed the bag. "Keep the change." The yellow rice and peas made Hoop think about his mother. He missed her Spanish dishes. "I love you ma." Hoop said kissing the back of his hand.

Bones saw Hoop's mink coat and reached in his back pocket. He grabbed the ski-mask, threw it on his face, pulled out the .357, raised his arm and squeezed the trigger.

"BOOM, BOOM."

The slugs crashed into the glass plated window of the restaurant shattering it. Hoop ducked, reached in his coat, pulled out the twin .40's and hid behind a wall. He looked over at the Dominican female and winked.

Bones stood in the middle of the street next to Menace. Hoop saw the red Miami Heat fireball logo on the ski-hat and nodded his head. He crouched down, made it to the shattered glass and raised his right hand.

"BOOM, BOOM, BOOM."

Bones ducked as shots whizzed past him. Menace returned fire with his .357.

"BOOM. BOOM. BOOM."

Hoop laughed, popped up and squeezed both guns. "BOOM, BOOM, BOOM, BOOM, BOOM. BOOM."

Hoop backed away, turned, hopped over the counter and made his escape through a back exit. He placed both hammers back in the holsters and ran through a few backyards that led him to his armored Maserati. He picked up his cell phone and called the only nigga he could trust. Spanish Dan answered on the third ring. Hoop told him to make his rounds, collect the money from all the project hustlers that he supplied with dope and then meet him at the executive lounge at Logan International Airport.

"I'm going back to Miami." Hoop said.

Chapter 38

Hoop laughed at the futile attempt on his life as he drove to his pent-house condo in Rollings Square. He drove down Washington Street, took a turn onto Harrison Ave. and pulled into the curved cobblestone driveway of the 184-unit complex. He stopped at the center island and thought about the grudge he had with the Barton family.

"Ma! I'm going to make each and every Barton pay for this," He said, as he continued driving. Minutes later he pulled into his reserved parking space in the underground garage.

Hoop was one of the best thinkers in his project and knew that the Barton and Taylor clans would take Bones' side. He needed to take a vacation down to Miami and relax. The only one he could trust these days was his man Spanish Dan. He stepped out of the car and took the elevator to the sixth floor.

Hoop purchased the condo for 750,000 dollars and invested another 175,000 into lacewood paneling for the foyer and den. He had carved out a paneled dining room with built-in stash spots and a marble fire-place.

Hoop stepped into the tumble-marble foyer that had New Zealand lacewood paneling. He looked up at the painted gold leaf and then at the gigantic baby picture of his mother, taken when she lived in Bogota, Colombia. He took off his mink, placed it in the closet and walked out of the foyer into an oak-floored dining room. He emptied his pockets, placed the credit cards and stacks of hundred-dollar bills on the glass table and took a left into the kitchen. He walked straight to the sub-zero fridge and grabbed a carton of pineapple juice. He poured a glass of juice and sat at the bi-level island and lowered his head. A tear came down his face.

All the thoughts of what had transpired were becoming too much for him. He raised his head and vowed to kill anyone associated with Bones. The vibration of his phone snapped him back to reality. He looked down and saw Lynn's number and declined the call. It vibrated again and he declined again. He had no conversation for her. He pulled out his other phone and dialed Spanish Dan's number.

"Yo!"

"What's good?"

"The count is Ninety-Seven stacks." Spanish Dan reported.

"Good, we are going on a vacation down bottom."

"The bottom?" Spanish Dan asked, confused.

" Yeah! The sunny MIA."

"Word, I have never been to Miami before."

"First time for everything. Meet me at the executive lounge at Logan Airport in two hours." Hoop said and hung up the phone.

Miami was Hoop's second home. The millions that he had made in Boston were laundered into various businesses in Miami and other parts of Southern Florida. He had all types of condos on South Beach, Miami Beach, Hialeah and Kendall. He owned many businesses: massage parlors, travel agencies, a plumbing company, a welding company, an electrical maintenance company, a bar on Ocean Drive and an upscale unisex salon.

Hoop informed Spanish Dan what happened with Bones before they relaxed. He wanted to take him out of his habitat and study his response. He decided to take a shower and clear his thoughts. While in the shower he decided to kill both Bones and Menace, but he wanted to wait a while and allow them to get their shine for a few years and then come and strike when they both least expected. He stepped out of the shower and grabbed the remote, hit the secret code and watched as the wall parted revealing a safe. He hit the combination to the safe and watched it open to reveal stacks of hundred-dollar bills. The money was shrink wrapped into thirty 100 thousand-dollar stacks. He grabbed one, tossed it on the bed and then walked to his closet. He had his closet decorated by the seasons. He had the chinchillas, Rex Rabbits, minks in

186

one corner. Leather jackets, suede coats, wool pea coats and snorkels were in another corner. He hit a button and a secret door opened up and he walked into the adjoining room where all his silks, lined, straw hats and cotton V-neck shirts hung on racks. He grabbed a pair of white Maury gator sandals. He stepped into the master suite, reached on the racks that hung on the wall near one of his three dressers and grabbed a diamond Franco chain that had a customized Boston Celtics medallion' with black, green and clear diamonds. He tossed the chain around his neck, reached in his drawer, grabbed a matching bracelet and snapped it on his wrist. He grabbed the 100 thousand dollars and placed it in a Louis Vuitton bag, walked to the living room and dialed his chauffeur's number.

Hoop walked to the window and watched all the activity in the SOWA District. He saw his ride, took the elevator downstairs to the underground garage and slid in the rear seat. He poured himself a glass of Louie XIII and took a sip. He watched the airport come into view and as he crossed over the Zakim Bridge. He looked at his iced-out Harry Winston watch: "45 minutes to kill."

The car pulled up to the airport. He poured one last glass of cognac, guzzled it and then opened the door. He stepped out, looked up at the darkening sky and then headed into the terminal.

Twenty minutes later Spanish Dan walked into the lounge. Hoop was one of three people in the secluded lounge on the top floor of the airport. He saw Hoop at the bar with a bottle of Nectar Imperial and walked over toward him. Hoop turned and laughed at Spanish Dan's cocaine white ankle length mink coat.

"Where are you going to Alaska?"

Spanish Dan saw how Hoop was dressed and knew he wasn't dressed for the sunshine state. He passed him a bag of money. Hoop opened the travel kit, looked in it and then passed it back to him.

"That's gas money."

Spanish Dan smiled at Hoop and knew they were going to have fun in Miami. He took a seat next to Hoop and opened the bottle of Moet and asked. "What's your net worth?"

"Seven million," Hoop lied. It was more like 13.5 million in cash and another 20 million in assets.

Spanish Dan almost choked on the Moet he was sipping. He looked over at Hoop and knew he was every bit of a multi-millionaire.

The next twenty minutes they sat and versed about their up-coming vacation. Over the P.A. system they heard their plane was boarding. Hoop got up and walked toward the door. Spanish Dan followed him. Hoop laughed once again at the mink coat, as they walked inside the terminal. Hoop stopped, turned around and curled his finger.

"Give me that mink."

Spanish Dan emptied his pockets and passed the coat to him. Hoop walked up to a young Spanish girl.

"What's your name?" Hoop asked in Spanish.

"Maria." She smiled.

"Nice name. My mother's name was Maria," He said thinking of his late mother and passed the young girl the mink coat, "Happy birthday Maria," he said, turning around and walking toward the ticket holder.

Chapter 39

A few days after the shooting Bones summoned all the Heath Mob and the elders to the Hennigan School yard for a meeting. The first members to walk into the yard was the Taylor clan. Bones smiled at his cousins: Castro, Lazy, Red Hawk, Junior and Ox. Even the older heads Essie Taylor came out to listen to his young cousin. Next was Ice, Belly, Saturday Night Rick, Freak, Miguelito, Spoon and Jessie. They were from the second generation of the Heath Mob. They hugged the Taylor Clan and gave dap to Bones, Menace, Skate and Skitzo. The twins, Clarence and Terrence came through the school yard from the Walden Street side alongside Art, Manny and Little Man from the Barton Clan. The last two to come were Forty-Five, Lenny Johnson and Harry Jones. They were the project elders from the infamous stick-up crew "Heat Makers."

Bones started off explaining his reason for shooting at Hoop. The faces of a few Heath Mob showed discomfort but they remained silent until it was their turn to speak. Bones knew there would be mixed emotions and one day he would have to face Hoop and handle his business. Bones spoke about how Hoop had betrayed Orchard Park. They all listened in silence and waited until he was finished. The first one to speak was the elder Forty-Five.

"The only reason why you are still here breathing and not flying from a project roof with a bullet to your head is because you are the son of Alfred Taylor."

"If he wasn't a Taylor then what?" Clarence defended his nephew.

"He would be flying from a roof-top." Forty-Five answered.

"If Hoop had any blood brothers instead of six sisters there wouldn't be any meeting, because the project would have been at war and both sides would have been soaked in blood." Saturday Night Rick said.

"That shit Hoop done with Orchard Park was some bitch shit." Freak blurted out.

"That did put us in harm's way and our bond with O.P. on threads," Red Hawk Taylor said.

"Let's talk about money. What about the projects that we are controlling?" Lazy asked.

"We have to abandon them because we don't have the connection nor the supply to keep feeding the hustlers that Hoop fed," Bones answered.

"Since Hoop ran all the dope fiends away, where are we going to make money?" Red Hawk asked.

"We have to build our project back to how it was when my uncle Greenback was alive," Bones looked his older cousin in the eye.

"I'm with it because there's no place like home," Art Barton spoke up.

"Here comes Orchard Park." Bones said, as he pointed to Itchy and what looked like about a half of dozen Orchard Park members.

Itchy led the way in a black leather suit with the words "United Project Syndicate" scrawled across the back in red letters. They came inside the lot and gave pounds and hugs. Itchy was looking like a million dollars with red diamonds on his wrist, neck and pinky.

"I like that leather outfit," Red Hawk said.

Itchy turned around and showed the words scrawled on the back so that the Heath Mob could read it.

"United Project Syndicate," Skitzo read. "What's that supposed to mean?"

"T-Price from the Mission Hill Project came down to Bumpy Road and asked us if we wanted to be part of a movement of uniting all the housing projects together. I listened to him and agreed that Orchard Park would join. This is the reason why we are here: to offer the same to the Heath Mob.

"I don't see why not. We fuck with T-Price and those niggas." Lazy said.

The next ten minutes they spoke about Hoop's betrayal and about how they would continue to make money together and bring money back to the project.

Chapter 40

**Lord forgive him, he got them dark forces
in him, but he also got a righteous cause
for sinning. Them a murder me, so I got to
murder them. First emergency, doctors
performing procedures, Jesus, I ain't
trying to be facetious, but
"vengeance is mine"**

- Lucifer

Jay-Z

Bones stood in the hallway of a building on Walden Street. The snow had yet to hit hard and the chilly weather had the hustlers playing the hallways. He watched Alesia's son Tragdon walk by dribbling a basketball.

"Hoop dreams, huh?" Bones opened the door and asked him.

"Yeah!" Tragdon answered.

"Follow your dreams and don't let nothing get in your way or get them shattered." Bones said, as he walked out of the hallway toward Tragdon. He grabbed the ball and looked at it. "Spalding, huh? Good basketball." Bones commented. "What court are you going to?"

"The one on the Old Side." Tragdon said, walking away dribbling the ball.

Ten minutes later Bones saw his twin cousins Myami and Nyami walking through the project. He got their attention and waved them over. They made their way toward him and gave a hug and a kiss. Bones pulled out some money from his front pocket and passed each of them a couple thousand dollars.

"That's for the first and last month's rent."

The twins took the money, placed it in their pockets and walked away. Bones knew everybody had a purpose in life and the twins' purpose was to get him two apartments around the area that H-Block controlled. He chose Homestead and Harold Street. He decided to move into their territory so he could have a greater chance of murdering them.

Bones watched the twins disappear and walked toward the basketball court. He stopped at the fence and watched Tragdon practice his ball handling skills. "Dribble behind your back while looking toward the sky for two minutes."

Tragdon looked at Bones and started dribbling behind his back. He kept losing his handle and became frustrated.

"Don't get frustrated, just do it." Bones coached.

It took Tragdon ten times to get it right. Thereafter, he started dribbling behind his back with ease and a smile came across his face.

"Good," Bones clapped. "Now dribble behind your back while walking from one end of the court to the other."

Tragdon became intimidated by the length of the court, but he still tried. The first six times he kept losing his handle at half-court and again became frustrated.

"If this is your dream, then do as I say and stop becoming frustrated." Bones barked.

Bones coached Tragdon for the next 45 minutes and was starting to have flashbacks of how hard Mr. Thibodeau was on him. Bones stepped back a few feet and bumped into his cousin Myami.

"Why do you have him practicing so hard in the cold?" Myami asked.

"It's his dream."

"Here go the keys," Nyami said, passing Bones both sets of keys.

"Thank you," Bones said, turning back to Tragdon. "PRACTICE MAKES PERFECT." Bones shouted, walking away.

Bones walked to the parking lot and opened the door to a rental car and slid in. He reached under the seat and pulled out a 100 shot .22 Calico Machine Gun. He placed the gun on the passenger seat, put the car in drive and pulled off.

The apartment that Nyami got for Bones was on Homestead Street. This was a known hang-out spot for H-Block. The past few weeks he drove through, studying their hangouts. He parked on Ruthven Street, hopped out, climbed a fence and crept through an alley.

Outside the building a few young gang members wearing Houston Astros varsity coats and ski -hats were congregating.

"*I have to clear the block to get into my apartment,*" Bones thought. He stepped a few feet forward, raised the Calico and pulled the trigger. The first wave of shots hit the ground and skipped across the pavement. "Fuck!" He cursed, remembering that he had to hold the Calico slightly upward. About time he lifted the Calico they were gone. "Next time," Bones mumbled, stepping out of the alley. He raised the pistol in the air and fired off.

The next few days Bones sat in the living room of his apartment on Homestead Street, staring out of his front window. He was watching H-Block as they hustled outside. He saw them stash guns in the alley, under car tires and behind buildings. When the police came and cleared the block, Bones made his way outside and stole their guns and was ready to use their weapons against them. He had yet to see Hitler. He knew she was the only H-Block member who knew his face. He took his beef with H-Block seriously. His amputated leg was a reminder of why he hated them so much. He wanted to take a trip to his other apartment on Harold Street. He waited until the block cleared and then made his move. He cut through a few back streets and saw a bunch of two-family houses on Harold Street. He took out his key, walked up the stairs to one of the houses and opened the door. He entered the house, sat on a crate and looked out the window. He reached in his pocket, grabbed a fist full of .22 bullets and started reloading the Calico.

Bones planned to put the fear of God in H-Block for the next few months. He figured once he was done H-Block would be a thing of the past. The only people who knew where he was at were his cousins who had rented the apartment for him. Both apartments that he had rented were perfect because they were directly in the areas where H-Block were known to hang. He had an advantage as he learned by watching the cars they drove, faces of members of the gang and where they stashed their weapons. Every chance he had he crept outside and either shot at them or stole their guns and drugs. The drugs he gave to his cousins to sell in Heath Street and the guns he planned to use on them.

"I'm going to let these bitch ass niggas breathe for a couple of weeks then its back on." Bones said, as he got up from the crate and walked into the living room, turned on the T.V. and waited for the news to come on.

Chapter 41

The pressure that Bones had been putting on H-Block since he had moved in their neighborhood made the police ramp up their presence. They had police cars parked everywhere that H-Block were known to control.

Bones walked to the fridge and opened it. He saw that he needed a carton of milk. "Damn, I need some milk," He said, as he walked to the window and saw that the street was empty. He grabbed his coat, ski-hat and left the apartment. He walked to a store on Humboldt Avenue. He saw that the police were gone and walked inside of the store. He went straight to the milk section and grabbed a gallon of low-fat milk. He held the gallon in his hand and walked to the front. He stopped and spotted a Houston Astros hat being worn backwards. He slightly turned and placed the milk near the chip rack.

The door to the store opened and a few females walked in talking loudly. He listened as they screamed "Predator's" name.

"Predator, when did you come home?" One of the females asked, hugging him.

"A couple weeks back. I had to spend a little time with my family before I got back to business. I see there has been a lot of action around here." Predator said, looking the girls in their eyes.

"Yeah! It's been a lot of shooting back and forth around here. Every-one is getting locked up," one of the girls said.

"Well, all you need to know is I'm back out here."

Bones felt his heart jump. The nigga with the Houston Astros hat was the one who had shot him and ended his basketball career. "*This nigga shattered my dream.*" He thought, as he stared at Predator to get a clear look at his face. *"Always look a man in his eyes before you kill him."* He said to himself.

Predator was fresh home from beating an attempt murder charge. He had been arrested on a warrant a few days after he had shot Bones.

"I'm glad that you are back," One of the girls said, "now give me ten dollars?" The female asked.

Predator reached in his pocket and pulled a few bills and passed her ten dollars. He wanted to say something smart to the female about being money hungry, but he decided to roast her another time.

"Thank you." The girl said, giving him a hug.

"Anytime, I'd do anything for the home team."

Bones hand shook as he held the gallon of milk. He decided to put the milk back after watching Predator walk toward the door.

"Predator wait for us," one of the girls said.

The girl that Predator gave the money to paid for her items and walked out of the store with him. Bones followed them out of the store and pulled out his gun.

"I'm not going to let no one mess this up." Bones thought, as flashbacks of Predator snatching the door open and shooting inside the van ran through his head. "This nigga tried to kill me." Bones mumbled.

Bones learned from his cousins to never shoot a man in his back. He always looked a man in the eye before he killed him. He wasn't taking no chances this time because it was personal. Bones clutched the pistol grip and raised the gun. "PREDATOR." He yelled.

Predator lowered his hand and attempted to reach in his waist just as Bones fired his gun.

"BOOM, BOOM, BOOM."

The first three shots missed Predator and the young girls. Bones fired off two more shots. Predator grabbed the female who had asked him for money as a shield. Bones tried to get a clear shot and fired twice more striking the girl once. Predator dropped her, pulled out his gun and smiled.

"Now it's a fair exchange." Predator said, raising his gun and firing off.

"BOC, BOC."

Bones ducked and ran behind a car. Predator walked into the street and fired off two more rounds.

"BOC, BOC."

Bones got from behind the car and stood in the middle of the street. It was just them two with blazing guns. Predator laughed and raised his hammer but Bones fired off first.

"BOOM, BOOM."

The first shot lifted Predator off his feet. Bones walked over to him and as he crashed to the pavement, he lowered the gun to his face. "This is for shooting me," Bones said before pulling the trigger. "BOOM." Bones walked over to the female who was shot, reached in his pocket and grabbed a twenty-dollar bill. "Are you money hungry?" He asked, stuffing the bill in her mouth and lowered the gun to her face. "BOOM. BOOM."

The girl's brains flew all over the pavement. Bones walked to his apartment and waited for the ambulance to come pick up his victims. He cleaned all his prints off his other guns and stashed them in boxes of paper that he had stacked in the corner. He picked up his cell phone, called his cousin Myami, told her to break the lease and pick him up. Next he called his mother.

"Hey ma!"

"What's up boy? Where have you been at?"

"I've been spending time with a female friend and trying to stay away from the project."

"Are you coming to the Christmas party in Bromley-Hall?"

"When is it?" Bones asked.

"This weekend."

"Yeah! I'll be there." Bones said. He spoke a few more words to his mother and then hung up. "Bromley-Hall huh. I will be there." Bones said, as he walked to the window and waited for his cousin to come and pick him up.

Chapter 42

Bromley-Hall was packed as everyone in the project came out to enjoy the Christmas Party. This was Bones' first-time spending with those in his project in a festive mood.

"Look at Nivea," Snake pointed to a female dancing on the dance floor.

"She's thick," another member named Jackal said, as he stared at Nivea's round derriere.

"Hey Bones," A female waved, as she walked past Bones and his Heath Mob crew.

"What's up Red-Dot? Every time I see you it seems like you are getting prettier and prettier," Bones said, as he was impressed with her skin that seemed to look golden, her-curvaceous body and long stringy hair.

Everyone was in a festive mood besides Menace. He still felt a certain way toward Speedy for leaving Juicy to die. He looked at Speedy and said to himself. *"This bitch nigga got to go."* He walked over toward Speedy. "Speedy let's go outside and smoke an L." He said, as he tapped Bones on the shoulder and leaned toward him. "Take a walk with me and this bitch ass nigga."

They walked outside and Menace turned around to Speedy. "Let's take a walk to Horan Way and blow this Dour." Menace said as he flashed a bag of Sour Diesel. They walked to 49 Horan Way and opened the project door and stepped inside the hallway. Menace reached in his back pocket and pulled out a pack of Backwoods and passed it to Speedy.

Speedy started cracking the blunt down the middle. They watched him empty the tobacco onto the floor.

"Yo! Speedy. We are about to put in some work. We need you to be the driver," Menace said, as he put his hand in his pocket.

"Yeah! You got that." Speedy answered, putting the finishing touches on the blunt.

"If something goes wrong are you going to leave us like you did my nigga Juicy?" Bones snarled.

Speedy heard the angry tone in Bones' voice and slowly looked up. The sight of the .45 handgun that Menace held in his hand caused him to piss on himself. Right then and there that's when he knew he was marked for death. "I didn't," Speedy tried to talk.

Before he could finish his sentence, Menace stepped forward and raised his .357. "The Heath Mob said your time expired." He laughed, as he pulled the trigger.

The .45 slug crashed into Speedy's forehead pushing him backward onto the floor.

A Heath Mob member named Skitzo was on the third-floor landing in the hallway snorting heroin. The past few months he had been secretly snorting the drug with an older female he was having sexual relations with named Asha who happened to be part of the Taylor Clan and Bones' first cousin on his father side. He heard the loud gunshot and dropped the bag of heroin on the floor. He stood up, looked down toward the lower level and saw Bones.

Bones pulled out his gun and walked up on Speedy as he twitched on the ground and pointed his .45 at him and pulled the trigger. The shots from Bones' .45 made the twitching stop. Menace tossed on the hood of his black snorkel coat and he and Bones walked out of the hallway and rejoined everyone in Bromley-Hall.

Chapter 43

The murder of Speedy made the project hot as fish grease. All the hustlers hustled cautiously. After the murder the Boston Police launched an intense investigation into the murder of Speedy. Mr. Homicide had a hunch that the murder of Speedy was an inside job and he had vowed to get those responsible for the murder. He directed the detectives Red Beard, Cheetah and Spikey to see what information they could gather around the Bromley-Heath Street Project. The only two people who knew were Bones and Menace and they intended to keep it that way.

Skitzo was on his way to Centre Street with a mouth full of twenty rocks of crack. He was still in disbelief that Bones had murdered Speedy. He knew Bones was nothing to mess with, but killing another member of the crew is one thing he never thought Bones would do. *"Bones is one crazy ass nigga,"* Skitzo thought, as he saw a few fiends standing near the basketball court at Jackson Square. "OOHH, WOOHH," He signaled to get their attention.

The fiends heard the hood call and waved him over. They pulled out their money as he approached them. He made quick exchanges with the fiends and started to walk away.

A Black Bronco turned onto Centre Street. Spikey spotted a drug deal near the basketball court. He pointed to where Skitzo stood with his hand out. Red Beard stopped and let Cheetah out of the truck and then sped forward and jumped over the curb.

Skitzo heard the loud motor, looked up and saw the Bronco. He ran toward the train station, but was chased down by Cheetah. He tussled with the detective for a few minutes. Red Beard came up and clocked Skitzo in the head with his flashlight. As Skitzo fell to the ground six pieces of crack came out of his mouth. He was placed in cuffs and escorted to the police precinct. When he came out of his unconscious state he was surrounded by the department's worst detectives. He tried to move but his right arm was handcuffed to the table.

"We are going to refer this case to the federal government, Mr. Homicide said with a grin.

"Federal government?" Skitzo asked, confused.

"Yeah! The Feds. This is your third crack charge and a conviction would land you in prison for the rest of your life."

"You can't fool me, I'm only twenty-one years old."

"Have you ever heard of the Three Strikes Law?" Mr. Homicide informed.

"Yeah!"

"Well this is your third strike with crack cocaine."

Skitzo thought about his last two distribution convictions and realized that it would be his third strike. At 21 years old it would be hard for him to do a life sentence with no kids and money to support himself. "I know who killed Speedy."

"Now we are talking," Mr. Homicide said as he pulled out a notepad, tape recorder and a pen.

The next six hours Skitzo gave them everything they needed to know about the murder of Speedy. He also told them about other crimes that happened around the project and even agreed to help infiltrate the Heath Mob.

Mr. Homicide picked up his phone and called the district attorney with the information they received. They booked Skitzo on a lesser charge of possession of crack cocaine and then escorted him to a holding cell.

Chapter 44

The grand jury testimony of Skitzo led to an indictment of Bones for the murder of Speedy. This was the first time in the history of the Heath-Mob that their code of silence was broken by a member.

Bones and other people from Bromley-Heath Street were watching two 13 & under teams play in the Maria Caicedo league inside the gym at the Hennigan school. Bones was impressed by the dribble of young Tragdon. Bromley Heath's 13 & under team was playing against a team from nearby Mozart Park. The skills Bones taught Tragdon paid off, as he dribbled behind his back, passed a no-look pass to his teammate and then raced across to the three-point line. His teammate saw him open and passed the ball. Tragdon caught it and shot the three pointer.

"MONEY, MONEY." Mercedes yelled.

Alesia smiled at her son's skills, turned toward Bones. "Thank you for teaching my son the art of playing basketball. Have you ever thought about coaching?"

"Nah! It would bring back many memories." Bones said, as he stared into Red-Dot's pretty eyes.

Alesia stared back into Bones' eyes and smiled. She turned back to the court and saw her son score another basket.

"I'm not sure if I will ever coach, but when I see potential, I will do as much as I can to help out. I was once a man of potential," Bones laughed.

"What are you laughing at?" Red-Dot asked.

"Nah! I was just thinking about something I did in the past."

"Oh!" Red-Dot said.

"Do you still work for my grandmother?"

"Yes!"

The clapping and cheering made Bones turn toward the game. He saw that Tragdon's defender was slow to get up.

"HE WAS LEFT HOLDING HIS ANKLE," A project kid named Dinero shouted.

* * * * * *

Red Beard took the turn down Heath Street and drove toward the project. Bones Red-Dot, Mercedes and a few others from the project were leaving the game. As they walked inside the project Mercedes saw the Bronco heading toward them.

"D-BOYS." Mercedes shouted.

Bones turned around and started walking the opposite direction. He heard the Bronco coming his way, turned and looked as it came up the high sidewalks of the project. He reached in his waist and tossed a black .9mm Taurus under a parked car.

The detectives didn't see Bones toss the gun under the car. Cheetah opened the door, hopped out like a ninja and ran toward Bones. Bones walked around the corner and kept walking through the project. He looked back and saw the detective race around the corner shouting.

"FREEZE. FREEZE, BOSTON POLICE."

Bones froze and lifted his hands in the air. The detective ran up on him and grabbed his left arm.

"What am I getting arrested for?"

"Murder one."

"Don't worry, I'll be home in thirty days." Bones boasted.

The detective marched Bones around the corner where several members of his crew and nosey neighbors now emerged. Bones looked at Tragdon and shouted. "PURSUE YOUR DREAMS."

Tragdon nodded his head and made an H with his fingers and flashed it at Bones.

Chapter 45

Hoop was shopping at the boutiques along Ocean Drive. He was with his P.I.C. (Partner in Crime), Spanish Dan. On their arms were two of the prettiest and wealthiest Colombian sisters in Southern Florida.

Damaris Blanco was Hoop's fiancé. She was a distant cousin of the late notorious Griselda Blanco (Black Widow). Damaris and her sister both had dark skin, stringy hair and petite hourglass frames. There were two things that set the sisters apart: Damaris's height and Rosanna green eyes. Damaris was a year older and took to modeling at a young age. When she was 20 years old, she was runner-up in the annual Miss. Colombia beauty pageant. While Damaris was competing in beauty pageants in Medellin her little sister became part of the police force. Over time she became crooked and quit and started to work for the AUC, a right-wing paramilitary group. The sister's older brother was in the drug game and it was he who had given Hoop the cocaine plug he needed.

Hoop laundered his money through Damaris' South American connections and his extended family. He invested in a disco club called "Casino Nites" in Barranquilla and a lounge he named after his late mother called "Maria's Lounge." He also became part owner of one of Bogota's soccer teams. The rest of his fortune was in overseas accounts in Grenada, Switzerland, and the Cayman Islands.

Hoop introduced Spanish Dan to Rosanna and they instantly hit it off. Hoop kept Rosanna's fortune a secret and told Spanish Dan that her wealth came from an inheritance of her late parents.

Spanish Dan fell in love with everything Miami had to offer: sunny weather, beautiful girls and luxurious living. The money that Hoop invested made his stay in Miami comfortable. Hoop had cocaine money coming from all directions in South Florida. He had the Haitians in Little Haiti and Palm Beach buying kilos, the Jamaicans in Overtown buying pounds and the Cubans in Hialeah buying multi-kilos weekly. He also had hustlers coming from Central Florida buying kilos. He shared most of his leisure time with his lady and her sister. He brought Dan to his studio that he had opened in an old storage facility and showed him the documentary that he was working on about Nate Lackland: one of Bromley-Heath legendary hustlers. He also had plans to make one about the stick-up crew, the Heat Makers, the original Heath Mob and Greenback's life story.

Hoop and Spanish Dan were ordering lunch at an outdoor cafe. He passed Damaris his Black Amex Card and sent her to get a few pairs of thongs, boy shorts and laced panties from La Perla. They watched the two sisters walk away.

"What hood nigga have a direct contact with a cartel?" Hoop thought, as he sat with his left leg crossed over his right. He had a few things to talk to Spanish Dan about. For the past months, he watched as Spanish Dan showed his undeniably loyalty to him and now it was time to tell him about what happened when Bones shot at him.

"The day we left Boston, Lynn's son Alfred and his boy Menace tried to assassinate me," Hoop began.

Spanish Dan scrunched up his face listening to Hoop explain the shoot-out in detail.

"I knew it was only a matter of time before we collided. The whole drama started when I approached him about playing for the Heath Mob basketball team. I came to him as an elder and he laughed like he was bigger than the team. He was a peasant. I could have easily had him shot dead in the project and a rose placed on his chest, but out of the respect I have for his grandmother's reputation I gave him a pass. The more I think about the situation, the more I want to react. I made my mind up two nights ago. I feel like I took a short and you know the Commissioner never takes losses, only gains."

"We could go back and bury that little nigga alive," Spanish Dan barked.

"Haste is not necessary," Hoop advised to Spanish Dan.

"Yes, it is."

"Patience is virtue. We'll give him time to get comfortable and then we strike when his guard is down."

"When he least expects huh? What's sixty-five percent out of forty?" Spanish Dan asked.

"Twenty-two and a half why?"

"Four more years, Bones father would be home from prison." Spanish Dan said.

"Oh! He'll be dead way before then." Hoop laughed, sipping on a bottle of champagne.

The next 45 minutes they both enjoyed champagne and their entrees. Damaris and Rosanna walked over to the table. In Damaris's hand was the most recent Boston Herald. She passed it to Hoop. He looked at the cover and read the caption.

"Star athlete arrested for grisly murder in Bromley-Heath Street project."

Hoop looked at the mug shot of Bones and laughed. He read the article and then passed the paper to Spanish Dan.

"I see since I left the project has been a mess. If I was there that would not have happened. I feel bad about the bad publicity Mrs. Barton's going to get for her idiot ass grandson."

Hoop knew that Speedy was marked for death since he left Juicy to die. It was hoop who kept the wolves from taking Speedy's life.

"We could still murder Menace." Spanish Dan grinned.

"Nah! I would rather make it a double funeral." Hoop smirked, popping another cork of Cristal.

Spanish Dan was one of Hoop's soldiers and anything Hoop said he would do. Spanish Dan knew that if he disobeyed Hoop, he would be swimming with the gators in a swamp in Gainesville, Florida.

Chapter 46

Bones was awaiting trial in Nashua Street on the sixth floor in the Murder Unit. The lawyer he had was a public defender. He knew his chances of winning with a public defender wasn't good. His family reached out to his former lawyer Gloria Curran. Over the years Gloria Curran's stock rose in the city, as she was known to beat high profile cases. Her asking price these days was 100 thousand for murder. The steep price put the Heath-Mob in a limbo as they hustled to get the money.

Bones sat on his bed thinking about the choices he had made in his life, how the impact of him being arrested for murder had on his mother and a few other things. The door opened and the correctional officer peeked his head in and told him he had a visit. He stood up and walked outside of his room, down the hall to the secluded visiting booth and opened the door. He was stopped in his tracks as he saw Hollis behind the thick partition plexi-glass. She was dressed in a purple blouse, light gray dress pants and a pair of gray Valentino heels.

Hollis found out that Bones was locked up from the same way the others found out: the media. She was hurt that he had gotten himself arrested for such a heinous crime. She decided to visit him to see how he was holding up and if he had needed anything.

"Hey Hollis, it's a surprise to see you in here. What you been up to?"

"Going to school, working, saving money and building my credit. What about you, how are you holding up in here?"

"I'm alright. I have my up and down days. Having this disability doesn't help at all."

"All you have to do is pray and have faith in God. Since the day I read about you being arrested in the newspaper it brought me back to the day when I dropped you off in Bromley-Heath. I knew from that scenery that it wasn't good for you. You've been through so much in your young life, this shows your true character and how strong you are. God willing that you make it out of here with your freedom. I have a question. What is your definition of choices?"

"Choices."

"Yeah! Choices. Because in this world we have choices and that's what you made to return back to the project."

Bones thought about what choices really meant. He wondered if killing Speedy on Menace's accord was a good choice. He looked at how beautiful Hollis was and knew if he had any shot at making her his queen, he had messed that up by making the choice and pulling the trigger on his friend. "I've been thinking about life and my purpose in it," he said, looking her in the eyes.

"What is your purpose?"

"My purpose was playing basketball and my stubbornness erased that dream. The day I got arrested I was watching the youth league and joy overcame me. I think my calling is to open a basketball camp and coach the youth and show them how to follow their dreams out of the hood."

"If you're serious, me and my family may be able to help you with some much-needed support. I'm willing to help support you in these trying times cause no one especially yourself deserves to be incarcerated. If this is what you want, I suggest that you should take a couple courses in sports nutrition and business finance."

"Why business finance?" Bones asked.

"Because it will give you the education you need to sufficiently operate your business. You said that you want to be a mentor to youth with helping them get out of the hood.'

"I understand." Bones said, "I just need to know which route I need to take to gain that education. Is the course a diploma or certificate?"

"Certificate. I want to work on getting you out of prison and completing your high school education. Are there any lawyers that you suggest?"

Yes. Gloria Curran is a family lawyer and one of the best there is in Massachusetts."

"Me and my mother will be paying Gloria Curran a visit to talk to her about how she can help you out."

"Call my mother and tell her whatever my friends have to give it to you." Bones said with a joyously smile. "Once I get through this, I promise to never return back to the street life. I mean that."

"I hope so Alfred, because there are people out here who love you and want the best for you. You never know if you get your act right and I'm single we can talk about what the future might hold." Hollis said with a wink and a smile. "I have to get ready to get out of here and I will write to you and stop by in the next couple weeks to follow up on our conversations." She said as she blew an air kiss, stepped up and walked away.

Bones walked out of the visiting booth and saw that there were a couple new faces in the unit. As he walked down the tier, he thought about the opportunities that Hollis offered him and knew if he played his cards right and ostracized himself from the streets they could live in peace. He walked to the television room and stepped in. He sat down and saw the McLaughlin twins warming up in their Duke Blue Devils uniforms.

"Soft motherfuckers." Bones mumbled, remembering the day he had scorched them for 57 points. He watched the first half of the game and was impressed by how the twin's game had progressed. He zoned out and became angry, as he thought about his disability. "*I'm supposed to be playing D-1 ball,*" he thought to himself.

"Yo! Those twins are from Mass," A nigga named Kill at will said.

"Yeah! Avon, Massachusetts," A nigga named Dawg confirmed.

"Avon. Where the fuck is that?" Kill at Will asked.

"In the North Shore." Dawg incorrectly said.

"Dawg, you're wrong. Avon is near Brockton." Bones corrected.

Bones watched the twins shoot their signature seventeen-foot jump-shot. It brought flashbacks to the first half of the only game he played against them and how he couldn't stop their post-game.

"Damn, they are doing it on the next level." He thought, as he watched the game. *"They are about to make it to the pros while I'm waiting to see if I will ever see the streets again."* He thought, as he turned around and walked out of the room. *"I need to really assess my future and leave this hood loyalty to Menace and the others."*

Chapter 47

The fear that Menace instilled in the Bromley-Heath project made him the most notorious member of the Heath-Mob. He was called the project's puppet master for the strings he pulled to make violent acts occur. His keen eye recruited the next breed of gangsters and created an oath for them: they would pledge allegiance to the Miami Heat fireball logo. He believed that children were the future.

Menace and Castro stood in an alley watching the parking lot on Heath Street. A black Mercedes pulled into the parking lot.

"Who's that?" Castro asked.

"Who knows? Let's see."

Hollis sat in the Mercedes listening to "I want my baby back home" by Keisha Coles. When the song ended, she reached in the back seat, grabbed her hand bag, took the keys out of the ignition and stepped out. As she stepped on the pavement, her Jimmy Choo heels almost crushed a used syringe. She shook her head at how loitered the parking lot was. She stared into the housing project that Bones called home. She was there to follow the order that Bones gave to deliver to Menace. She started walking toward the project.

"Yo! She must be a lawyer or private investigator," Castro said, eyeing Hollis.

"Come on let's see." Menace said, cutting through the alley. They hopped over a small wrought iron fence and ended up in front of a project building. They heard the sound of heels clicking as they neared the corner.

Hollis turned the corner and was stopped by the two gangsters dressed in black. She jumped a few feet back. The hairs on her spine stood straight up as she saw the cold look in Menace's eyes.

"I'm looking for a person they call Menace," her soft voice said.

"Who sent you?" Menace asked.

"Alfred Barton."

"My cousin Bones," Castro clarified.

Hollis looked at Castro, saw the resemblance and knew that he was indeed one of Bones' cousins.

"Yes," She answered.

"Who are you?" Menace stepped in her face.

"His lady." Hollis replied with authority.

"She got jokes," Castro said laughing. "Who are you?" Castro asked seriously.

"His lady, his sponsor, his girlfriend, his ticket out of the project and his future wife." Hollis replied with an attitude.

"What's your business in Heath Street?" Menace asked.

"Lawyer fees. I already put a Seventy-Percent down payment on his attorney fees. He sent me to ask Menace for the other thirty-percent."

"I'm Menace and Bones is my best friend. Anything he needs he shall receive. Follow me," He said, turning around and heading toward the New Side of the project.

Hollis followed him. The walk from the Old Side to the New Side took some mileage off her heels. It seemed like forever to reach Plant Court. As they turned a corner, she saw over two dozen gang members wearing Miami Heat caps.

"Wait here.' Menace said, leaving her with Castro.

While waiting she observed the buildings with windows so close to each other that the rooms inside had to be small. She saw littered side-walks, gangsters and dope fiends walking around aimlessly.

"I won't allow Alfred to come back here. This project is the worst," Hollis thought, as she watched heroin sales being made in the open and the sight made her turn her head. *"This is an open-air drug market."* She said to herself, as she looked at her chrome Patek Phillipe watched and started to get worried about her Mercedes being broken into. "Where is he at?" She asked Castro

"He'll be back."

"OOHH, WOOH!" Menace shouted from a third-floor window.

Hollis looked everywhere but up. Castro tapped her shoulder and pointed to the third floor of the project building. She looked up and spotted Menace waving her upstairs.

"Go. He's calling you." Castro said.

Hollis hesitated for a few seconds then stepped forward. She walked through the thick crowd of Heath Mob members.

"Two for twelve, two for twelve," A member shouted, marketing his product.

"Taster's Choice, Taster's Choice." Another yelled marketing his brand.

Hollis made it past the hustlers and felt relieved. She opened the hallway door, stepped in and paused. The strong smell of urine filled her nostrils. She held her breath as she looked at half of dozen older Heath Mob members crouched down playing a game of dice.

"Four, Five, Six." Someone yelled.

Hollis walked past them and up the stairs. She made it to the third floor and was spooked by Menace who had his hood over his head. She walked past him into an apartment. On a coffee table in the living room was a pile of cash. Menace closed the door and joined her in the living room. He looked at her and walked to the table.

"How much is thirty-percent?"

"Thirty thousand." Hollis said, reaching in her purse for her receipt. She pulled it out and passed it to Menace. "Here this is the receipt."

"No need for that. I always take care of my man. He is a solid dude who should be well taken care of. For one hundred thousand dollars who is he trying to get Alan Dershowitz." Menace joked.

"No! Gloria Curran." Hollis corrected him.

"Damn! Gloria made it to the hundred-thousand-dollar mark. She's worth it." Menace said as he finished counting out the money Hollis asked. He put the money in a bag and passed it to her.

"Tell Bones, whatever he needs just to holler the Heath Mob is at disposal."

Hollis reached out her hand for Menace to shake it. He looked at her and threw out three fingers.

"Around here we give three's," Menace said, introducing her to the three-finger handshake.

Hollis mimicked Menace's three fingers and touched his. They saluted each other and walked out of the apartment.

Chapter 48

Bones realized that his dreams of playing pro ball were shattered the day he had gotten shot. The only time he saw his mother smile was when he took Braintree High to the state championship. That was the last time he saw her smiling and the constant crying on the visits broke his heart.

"I'm not straying this time," Bones thought as he heard over the intercom his name being called for an attorney visit.

Bones finished reading the last few pages of the chapter about real estate, placed the book mark on his chapter and walked out of the cell. He saw Gloria Curran sitting behind a table in the attorney visiting room. She had her hair wrapped in a bun and a pair of Cartier glasses laid on the table. He opened the door, shook her hand and sat down. She slid him the police report and then looked him in his eyes.

"You might be able to figure out who the snitch is." Gloria Curran said.

Bones read the police report and couldn't figure out who gave the statement. It could have been anyone. He looked at her with a clueless expression on his face.

"Read this." She said, as she slid a thick stack of papers toward him.

Bones picked up the papers and realized they were grand jury minutes. He read the first ten pages and had a hunch that it was his childhood friend Skitzo. He wasn't 100% sure because the name was blacked out but his intuition told him that it was Skitzo. The limited vocabulary, age and other information all pointed toward Skitzo. He finished the transcripts and looked at the death certificate, autopsy report and a few other witness statements regarding his case.

"This nigga Skitzo had committed treason," Bones thought. "Do you have an extra copy?"

"I would send you an extra copy tomorrow. It will arrive in a few business days.

"Perfect." Bones said. "Would they ever give me a bail?"

"In the coming months I will file a motion to request bail. Right now, is not the best time to request it because the judge on the bench is the worst when it comes to granting bail. Every six months the judges rotate and this is only his second month, so we have four months and then I will put the motion in. I advise you to continue taking courses, staying out of trouble and maintain good conduct with your family and if you could try to get some recommendation letters."

Bones agreed with her and he knew that the judge she was talking about was Arthur "Throw-a-way-the key" Nee and if he went up against him, he would definitely be denied bail. He looked at the Cartier glasses and liked her choice of eye wear.

"Here these are for you." Gloria said pushing the glasses toward Bones.

Bones picked up the rimless glasses and smiled. He looked back at his lawyer and she read his mind.

"Those are from your wife

"Wife?" Bones asked perplexed.

"Yes! Your wife."

Bones felt blessed that Hollis claimed him as her husband. He placed the glasses on his face, shook his lawyer's hand, and walked out of the room. *"This nigga Menace better get rid of Skitzo's rat ass before this is all over or I'm going to bring it to him and show him who the real boss of the Heath Mob is."*

Chapter 49

Hollis lived in a nice diverse community six miles west of Boston named Newton. Newton was ranked the second safest city in the United States according to Morgan Quinto's annual report of the safest and most dangerous cities. It was made up of 13 unique villages, each with its own downtown and post office. The pleasant community was perfect for her and Bones to live a nice, quiet life. She envisioned him and her holding hands while walking along the local lake.

The Median price for a house in Newton was $745,000. She lived in a Mediterranean style house a few blocks down from Boston College. Behind the house was a foot trail. She lived alone just her and her French poodle that she named Lexus. The house was a present for enrolling into medical school at Boston College. Her parents put a down payment and paid the mortgage for two years until she found steady employment to take over the payments.

Her phone rung as she sat in her car listening to music. She answered it and listened to the caller. It was the headmaster from Newton North High School. She listened and then put the car in drive and pulled off.

Ten minutes later she pulled up to the large campus and parked in an empty parking lot. She grabbed the keys from the ignition, opened the door and walked across the lot. She found an entrance, opened the door and followed the signs that pointed to the headmaster's office. She saw a display case filled with trophies and plaques. She walked toward it and stopped. The display case was lined with trophies in track, basketball and football. What stood out the most were the three basketball trophies. She looked at the newspaper clippings and stared to read them. The last name Barton piqued her interest. She instantly thought about

Bones' family. The name Raymond Barton kept popping in each article. She was impressed by the stats that he had put up in his three years of dominating the league. She started reading the last article and looked at the picture of him hugging his mother.

"Oh! My God," She said covering her mouth. "Raymond Barton is Bones' uncle." She stared at the picture of Mrs. Mary Barton for a moment, then turned around and walked toward the office. She knocked on the door and opened it. She greeted the headmaster and then sat down.

* * * * * *

Bones sat in his cell looking at the pictures that Hollis had sent him of her house in Newton. He knew the city well for it was where his late uncle Greenback went to high school. Bones could tell by the price of the house that Hollis's parent were rich. He hoped that they would approve of their relationship.

"Everyone's living their life while I'm waiting for a judgement that could land me in jail for a life sentence," He said. He became angry at Menace for granting Speedy's death wish. "I need to relieve some stress," he mumbled walking out of his cell toward the phones.

Hollis sat in the headmaster's office signing papers for her new job as a secretary in the psychology department. Her phone buzzed. She picked it up and saw Bones name on the caller I.D. "Excuse me, I need to take this business call," She said, as she walked out of the office. "Hello."

Hollis accepted the call. Immediately she heard the stress in Bones' voice and became worried. She informed him that she was at a job interview and that if she could make it to a night visit, she would be there. She spoke for a few more seconds, hung up and walked back into the office. "Are there any open coaching positions for the female basketball team?"

"Yes! There is an assistant coach job."

"I would like to apply for that as well. I have experience in playing basketball and a deep knowledge in coaching. Could I ask a question?"

"Sure."

"Who was the greatest basketball player in this school's history?"

"Raymond Barton. He was a METCO student from Jamaica Plain in Boston. I could still remember the years he had took us to three consecutive state championships." The headmaster smiled.

"Winning is definitely a team effort." Hollis said.

"He was the best at it. He always put his team first."

Hollis stood up, shook his hand and walked out of the office. She had two jobs and now she had to work on getting Bones out of prison and coaching a city league in order to gain enough experience to potentially coach the boy's team at Newton North.

Chapter 50

The next four months Bones matured into manhood. He became so entrenched in his courses that his dialogue was beginning to change. He added various business terminology to his vocabulary and was starting to use the business words that he was learning in his everyday dialect. He started teaching other inmates about business management. He spoke to the Sheriff and asked if he could teach a course in business. The Sheriff agreed and let him teach a small class of six inmates. The war stories he once told were a thing of the past, as were all the murders, shootings and mayhem he committed in the streets. The whole unit saw he wasn't the same Bones who came in nine months back and saw how he had grown since he been there.

Today he was going for a bail hearing. He met all the criteria that his lawyer had requested. He had earned his high school diploma, two certificates from Penn Foster, recommendation letters from his grandmother, Dr. Alexander, Hollis, Mr. Thibodeau and the Sheriff of the county. The Sheriff's recommendation included his clean record of disciplinary reports. He managed to stay out of trouble and became the head orderly in the unit.

"Barton, court," the correctional officer announced, through his intercom.

Bones rolled off the bed and got on his knees, clasped his hands together and prayed. In his prayer he asked the lord for bail. He opened his eyes, got off his knees, meditated for a few minutes and then brushed his teeth and washed his face. He looked out of his cell and saw other inmates in the common area waiting to be called for court.

Bones knew the judge's decision would either make or break him. In his mind he knew his criminal past would be brought up and with an attempt murder and two murder charges on his record his chance of a bail was up in the air. He grabbed his Cartier glasses, a manila envelope and opened the door. He made his way down to the flats and sat at a table. He looked at all the accused murderers and knew this was his last time in coming to prison. "I can't do this no more."

They walked out of the unit and down stairs to the dressing room and was stripped by a correctional officer. Another officer passed Bones a brown paper bag that contained his court clothes. He opened it and pulled out a white dress shirt, a pair of tan slacks and matching white and tan dress shoes.

The ride to Suffolk County Courthouse was short. Bones was placed in a cell and was stripped off of his cuffs. He shared the cell with three other inmates. He sat in a corner and listened as they gave away their identities by telling war stories.

Two hours later Bones was called. He stood up, walked to the door and was cuffed and escorted to the courtroom. Minutes later the door popped open and Bones saw a few members of his family, Mr. Thibodeau, Dr. Alexander, and Hollis. The court officer took off his cuffs and escorted him inside of the courtroom. He walked over to his lawyer and sat down.

"We have a good judge." His lawyer whispered.

"Who?" Bones asked.

"Mrs. Wall."

Bones' prayers were answered. He prayed hours earlier that he hoped to face Mrs. Wall.

The Honorable Catherine Wall was most lenient judge in Massachusetts. She was known to release some of the worst criminals in state history. She mostly always favored in the defendants corner.

Bones watched the judge walk out of her chamber and took her seat on the bench. The next twenty minutes the judge listened to the district attorney blast Bones about his criminal past and being a threat to public safety. Bones lawyer took notes on the inconstancies in the district attorneys attempt to keep Bones in custody.

After the district attorney finished Gloria Curran got up and gave her statement how Bones was a product of his environment and how the project, he was raised in was cursed. She pointed out his disability, the false accusations of murder that he was being charged with and the juvenile attempted murder that she deemed as youthful mistakes. She passed over the recommendations, certificates from Bones' course and his progress report from the Sheriff of the Nashua County jail. The judge read the papers and looked over at Bones.

"Young man, since the age of twelve you have been committing murders. I read the report, listened to your character witnesses and never in my thirty years on the bench have I witnessed a progress report from a Sheriff. I feel that you took the steps to rehabilitate yourself while awaiting trial. You once had a promising dream of playing basketball that was shattered by bullets that left you disabled. Over the years I witnessed hundreds of wolves in sheep clothing. You are still young at nineteen and I'm pretty sure with the family support that I see here in the court that you would do the right thing. I do not want to detail your plans of furthering your education.

I do not agree with what the district attorney said about being a future threat to public safety. Those words were rather harsh for a young man your age. At nineteen you still have your whole life ahead of you. Young man, you have to understand that you have a disability that sidelined a potential successful career in basketball. I grant you a bail of one hundred thousand dollars cash bail, no surety. I prohibit you from returning to Suffolk County until after your trial." The Judge said, as she banged her gavel.

Bones lowered his head as tears streamed from his eyes. He looked over at his family with a smile. He knew any day he would once again be walking the streets of Boston, but this time he was pursuing another dream: college.

Chapter 51

I'm a bully with da bucks/ don't let
the patent leather shoes fool you youngin.
I have the fully in the tux, that was my past
I'm so grown up/ I don't have one Gun on me/
got a slum army that would hire a gun
army/ that would get you spun like laundry

Jay-Z

Hoop and Spanish Dan were on Damaris and Rosanna's brother's private Cessna Jet en route to Boston Logan's International airport. The sisters traveled in luxury whether by land, air or water. Their brother had two yachts, a jet, and countless luxury sedan. He was a multi-millionaire and his taste for exquisite things showed it. They were on their way to attend Bromley-Heath's annual Family Day in the project. It was Hoop's idea to return to the project he was raised in. He wanted to rub his wealth and taste for exotic women in everyone' face.

The plane landed and they stepped off. Outside on the tarmac was a white Rolls Royce limousine waiting to take them to the hotel. As they inched inside the limousine Rossana grabbed the remote and switched the 16 disk C.D. changer to Rick Ross's first album "Port of Miami." She looked over at Spanish Dan who had on black linen shorts, black silk shirt and a black Panama straw hat and smiled. "You look good in black." She said running her tongue through his ear.

The limousine pulled up to the Ritz Carlton hotel and Rossana stepped out in a black lace dress, ostrich Roberto Cavalli shoes with black diamond encrusted heels. She grabbed Spanish Dan's arm and they walked inside of the hotel.

* * * * * *

Menace funded nine of the sixteen grills for Family Day. He spoke to a few fishermen he knew from Maine and bought hundreds of lobsters, crabs, flounders, haddock, scallops and shrimp. He was proud to be the man he had become these days. Once he received the paper work with Skitzo name as a rat he made sure that no one earth would ever see or hear from him again.

The project rappers were performing on the makeshift stage for Family Day. The Femme Fatales had on Rest in Peace "Greenback" and "Juicy" t-shirts. Lynn was busy helping her family at one of the grills.

From the rooftop Tragedy saw the luxury limousine cruising down Columbus Avenue. The Rolls Royce took the turn up Centre Street and parked across the street from the project. Hoop was the first one to step out. He held the door open for his lady and waited for Spanish Dan and Rosanna to join them before they walked inside of the project.

Nyami was the first to spot Hoop. She walked away from the pack of Femme Fatales in search of her aunt Lynn. She found her talking to another family member and pulled her to the side. "Hoop is here."

"Where is he at?" Lynn asked.

Nyami pointed toward Jackson Square train station. Lynn looked and what she saw made her heart sink. She saw Hoop holding hands with the prettiest dark-skinned girl her eyes ever laid on. The diamonds that sparkled off her necklace and tennis bracelet made Lynn jealous.

Hoop walked over toward the Heath-Mob in a black tux, with a red Gucci tie and black patent leather shoes and tapped Red Hawk on the shoulder. "What's up partner?"

Red Hawk looked at him and then at the female on his arm. He hesitated and then spoke. "Living the Heath life."

"I hear that. I see the mob is still together in my absence." Hoop said sarcastically.

"Always, it's Heath Mob forever. What's up Dan?" Red Hawk said reaching over and giving Spanish Dan dap.

"I see there are a lot of new faces out here."

"When one falls ten more come out of the house." Red Hawk said, throwing a cheap shot at Hoop.

"Don't flatter yourself, I'm still a bully with da bucks, don't let the patent leather shoes fool you," Hoop said, opening his tux.

Alesia saw Hoop from apartment. A few minutes later she came out with a bag. Damaris looked over Hoop's shoulder while Rosanna looked over Spanish Dan's shoulder. It was Rosanna who saw Alesia coming over with a bag. Hoop was busy staring at Menace that he didn't see Alesia come over until he heard Rosanna's voice.

"Traffic."

Hoop turned and faced Alesia. "Red-Dot." He smiled, as he gave her a hug and a cheek kiss. "What's in the bag?" He asked, as he stared at the bag in her hand.

"The money I owe you from past business." She said, passing him the money. "That's the forty-seven thousand dollars I owe you."

Hoop passed the money to Spanish Dan and told him to make sure that each kid gets two hundred dollars. As Dan passed money to each kid, Hoop carried a brief conversation with Alesia. After Dan was done, Hoop turned to his crew. "Alright my niggas, I just came to pay homage to Mrs. Mary and to make sure my legacy was still intact."

"Hoop. The project misses you," Mercedes said hugging him.

"I know. Who doesn't miss the commissioner?"

Hoop saw Menace smirking. He looked at Rosanna, closed his eyes and then laughed. Rosanna eyed Menace fiercely she knew that he was marked for death.

Menace saw Hoop with his small crew and laughed, tapped a few of his little niggas and pointed. "You see that nigga, he's a clown. I ran him out of the project."

"What is he doing back?" A young nigga named Dinero asked.

"Who knows, but he won't make it out of here alive." Menace said.

Hoop walked up to Lynn's sister Lena and kissed her on the cheek. He looked at Lynn and shook his head. "Hi, Evelyn, this is my fiancé from Colombia. Isn't she beautiful?"

239

Lynn looked at the attractive Colombian and agreed that she was indeed beautiful. "She's pretty." Lynn admitted.

"I know. That's why she has been my number one for the past eight years." He said, turning around and walking toward Mrs. Mary and the rest of the T.M.C.

Mrs. Mary was sitting in a chair surrounded by many of the Tenant Management Corp. Menace's mother, Mrs. Johnson spotted Hoop and waved. Hoop made his way toward the heads of the project management.

"Hi, Jose. Mrs. Mary said, hugging Hoop.

Hoop hugged Mrs. Mary and went over and hugged Mrs. Johnson. Over her shoulder he watched her son Menace with a devilish smirk on his face. Hoop winked and kissed her on the cheek. "How is the grocery store?"

"It's doing good. Thank you, Jose. I appreciate all the contributions to the project that you have made in the past. There needs to be more people like you." Mrs. Mary responded.

Hoop introduced the T.M.C. to his fiancé and then turned and walked over to one of the grills. He picked up a burger and passed it to Damaris.

Lynn looked at the two sisters and felt ugly compared to their exotic looks. She knew that Hoop was a man of extreme taste and she blamed her son for shattering her dream of being happy in Hoop's arms.

Chapter 52

While the residents of Bromley-Heath were enjoying the festivities of Family Day, Bones relaxed with Hollis

on a beach in Cape Cod. He was far away from the drama and could care less what others were doing.

"I set up an appointment for you to take the S.A.T. back home." Hollis said.

"When?" Bones asked.

"Monday."

"Good, that gives us the whole weekend to ourselves."

"I love you." Hollis said as she laid her head on Bones' chest.

"No, you don't, you just love my sex." Bones playfully teased.

They spent the rest of the weekend studying for his S.A.T. prep exam, having sex, taking walks on the beach and enjoying each other's company.

Bones slept the whole ride back home. His light snoring was cute to Hollis as she sang the whole ride home. She pulled up to the parking lot of Newton South High School and parked. Bones woke up, looked at the large campus and asked. "Where are we at?"

"Newton South, the place where you are scheduled to take your S.A.T."

Bones kissed her on the lips, opened the door and stepped out and walked toward the entrance. He saw a crowd standing near a door. He followed them to the gymnasium. He stopped and looked at the name of the gymnasium. "Jose Caicedo Gymnasium" he read. His heart dropped as he remembered his last thought about his enemy. He couldn't believe the school named a gym after Hoop. He heard the rumors that Hoop donated a million dollars to the school years back, but didn't believe it. "*I guess Hoop is a rare breed.*" Bones said to himself.

Bones walked inside the gym and saw Hoop's name engraved in everything from the backdrop to the bleachers and his initials that were engraved at center court.

"What a lasting impression."

Bones walked over, registered his name and then went to the tables that were spread out in the gym. He felt butterflies and knew he had to get a high score to get into the National Honor Society.

Hollis sat on the patio watching her poodle run around in circles in the yard. Her phone rang. She picked it up and spoke to Bones' lawyer. Gloria Curran informed her that the judge granted the motion for a speedy trial and gave her the date. Hollis wrote down the date and then hung up.

Three hours later she pulled up to the parking lot. Bones saw his lady pull up and walked over toward the car. He opened the door, slid in and kissed her on the lips.

"I got some good news."

"What?" Bones asked.

"I spoke to your lawyer and we have a trial date in eight weeks."

"*The sooner the better,*" Bones thought, as he knew with Skitzo's body missing that the case would be an easy acquittal. "My results should be back in thirteen days."

Chapter 53

The past month and a half the homicide detectives cruised through Bromley-Heath looking for Skitzo. His mother had filed a missing person report and everyone who was related to him and the Boston police force was looking for him. The district attorney warned the police department that if they didn't find him that Bones' case would be a waste of taxpayers' money

Tragdon walked through the project when he heard someone call his name. He looked up at one of the project buildings and saw Asha waving for him to come upstairs. Tragdon lifted his Miami Heat cap and looked up at her window. He heard all the rumors in the project about her giving the best blow job and he had yet to explore too deep in the sex field. *"This might be my time to see what everyone is talking about."* He thought, as he made his way toward her building. He opened the hallway door and walked up the stairs. He stopped at her landing and saw that her door was cracked. He pushed it open and walked in.

Asha was waiting for him in the hallway in a red oversized T-shirt, no bra or panties. He walked over and gave her a hug and then walked inside of the living room. He watched as she lifted up the T-shirt and tossed it in the corner. His dick got hard at the sight of stretch marks on her stomach, droopy breast and a bushy vagina. She reached on the coffee table and grabbed a condom and ripped it open with her teeth, placed it in her mouth. Tragdon pulled down his pants and watched as she got on her knees and rolled the condom on his dick with her mouth. She used her hands and mouth to give him what she described as "her masterpiece". He exploded in less than a minute and she stood up and smiled at him. She knew the head game that she had just given him locked him down.

"It never fails." She said watching him walk to the bathroom to clean himself up.

Tragdon cleaned himself up and came back out to Asha opening a glassine bag. He watched as she emptied the brown powder on the table and divided it into two lines. She grabbed a rolled-up dollar and called him over.

"Watch this." She said.

Tragdon watched her as she snorted a line of heroin up her left nostril.

"Come on take a sniff. This shit will make your dick hard for hours."

"I'm good."

"You not a true Heat nigga. If you did you would test your product to see if it's potent."

"I don't sell heroin so there's no need for me to test anything."

"Like I said you not a true Heat nigga. If you did you would come and snort this with me you little bitch."

"Don't disrespect me."

"Well stop acting like one. All these niggas around her be sniffing on the low."

"Not Menace."

"You sound stupid. He's the biggest undercover dope fiend in the project." Asha lied.

Hearing his idol had been treating his nose made him want to try it. He grabbed a dollar bill, lowered his head and before he took a sniff, he raised his head and said, "I'm not going out like that."

"You're smart. You're going to last in the P, just don't let no one influence you to do anything you don't want to do."

Tragedy walked to her window and saw Menace walking his pit bull. He wondered if Menace was on cloud nine like Asha had described.

* * * * * *

Menace walked to his car, placed his pit bull in the passenger seat. He looked up and down the street and eased himself into the car. He popped in the Heath Life C.D. and listened to the projects greatest rappers.

Dressed in an all-black hooded sweat suit, Spanish Dan sprung out of the bushes and crept toward the driver's door. In his hand was a .40 caliber handgun loaded with Hollow Tips.

Menace put the car in drive and grabbed the steering wheel. The first slug from the silenced handgun crashed into the window shattering it in a thousand pieces. The bullet hit him in the temple. Spanish Dan pumped three more shots into the window. He snatched the door open and raised the gun to Menace's slumped body and pumped a few more shots and then pointed at the barking pit bull and silenced him. He backed away and slid into the darkness leaving Menace with his brains splattered all over his Mercedes Benz customized seats.

An hour after Menace was killed Bones' mother called him and told him. He was in disbelief that his friend was murdered. *"I'm done with the streets. I'm not even going to try to find out who had murdered my man. It will come to the light and get handled. The good thing is I passed the S.A.T. No Roger, no case. "I just need to rid myself of this case and go on and live my life."* What Bones didn't know was that Hoop was head hunting and next on Hoop's list was Bones. "I'm going to spend the next few weeks preparing for my court date and the rest is history" Bones said to himself as he looked across his front yard.

Chapter 54

Bones mourned the lost of his best friend Menace, but he. Vowed to never return to the streets. He knew with Menace's mindstate that there were only two outcomes: death or prison. He had his own demons he was facing.

Two weeks came fast for Bones today was the date of his decision for his bench trial with the judge. He sat in the car waiting for Hollis to join him. She walked to the mailbox, grabbed the stack of mail and joined Bones in the car. She saw that one of the letters came from Emory University in Atlanta, Georgia. She placed the letters in her purse and pulled off.

They pulled up to Suffolk Superior courthouse and parked on a side street. They got out and walked to the courthouse and took an elevator to the trial floor. Bones saw his family there and gave each one of them a hug. He walked over to his lawyer and saw that she had her game face on.

"The decision should be quick. I was able to use the judge's opinion as a road map and I did an excellent job at shaping the judge's view of the case. The key to all of this is that they have no witnesses and somehow, they can't find Roger and like I told you "No Roger, no case." The judge we have is fair and with no witnesses most likely the case would go in our favor."

"I hope so." Bones said, as he walked inside the courtroom with his lawyer and sat down at a table. He looked at all his family and friends piling inside the courtroom and he started to become nervous.

Unbeknown to Bones Daniel Levi, the orchestrator of the Barton's Law was sitting in the courtroom with a few of his Jewish politicians.

They were there to see the outcome of Bones murder case. Tucked under Daniel Levi's arm was the newest edition of the Boston Herald. Inside of the newspaper was a full-page article about convicted juvenile murder "Shyheim 'Scar' Carter" who was set to be released in a few days.

The judge came out and everyone rose to their feet. A couple seconds later they sat down and the court proceeding started. Bones looked over at Mr. Homicide and the other detectives with a blank stare. He knew they were frustrated that they couldn't find Skitzo. Bones knew that if he was to ever return to the streets of Boston that the police would be looking to arrest him for anything. He looked back at Hollis and saw that she was now joined by her mother. He smiled at them.

Mr. Homicide saw the happy look on Dr. Alexander's face and wondered where he knew her from. He looked at Bones with evil in his eyes as he listened to the judge speak about the history of the case.

An hour later the judge finally read his reasons on how the prosecutor didn't prove beyond a reasonable doubt that Bones was guilty.

"The court finds the defendant Alfred Barton "Not Guilty" of the charge of Murder in the first degree. This court is adjourned." The judge said as he banged his gavel, picked up his cat and disappeared into his chamber.

Cheers erupted in the courtroom, as everyone gave hugs. Bones turned to his lawyer and gave her a tight hug. He thanked her, shook her hand and looked in the crowd for his mother and Hollis. He found them hugging each other. He walked over toward them and Hollis passed him a letter. He opened the letter and saw that it was an acceptance letter to Emory University in Atlanta, Georgia. He couldn't hold back his joy and started to shed a tear. He passed the letter to his mother who gave a similar response. Lynn thanked Hollis and her mother for believing in her son and helping him change his life around.

"This is my ticket out of the hood." Bones said pointing to the letter. He turned around and saw a sour look on Mr. Homicide's face. He wanted to rub it in the detective's face, but decided not to. "That faggot will never see me again in the P." Bones said as he walked out to the lobby with his mother.

Bones heard his mother bragging to family and friends about him being accepted into medical school in Georgia. Alesia heard Lynn bragging and walked over to Bones, gave him a hug and congratulated him on being accepted into medical school. He walked over to his fellow Heath Mob members and gave each one them the three-finger salute and a hug.

"Cuddy, do me a favor and throw the H up one last time?" Red Hawk asked.

Bones made an H with his fingers and threw it up in the air the same way he had done when he took Braintree High to the state championship. He saw the three well dress politicians walk past him and wondered who they were. Bones spoke for a minute longer and then left the courthouse with his mother, Hollis and Dr. Alexander.

"After I go and see my grandmother then I will make my rounds to visit the family in the project and then it's our time." Bones said hugging Solange.

* * * * * *

Hoop and Spanish Dan sat across the street in a light blue Town and Country van with tinted windows. They watched Bones walk out of the courthouse with his entourage.

"Who's that with Bones?" Spanish Dan asked.

"It must be his defense team." Hoop said.

"Not holding hands like that."

Hoop put the van in drive and pulled off. He turned the corner and double parked next to a purple Dodge Magnum. Minutes later Alesia came around the corner and walked to the Magnum. She made it to her car and spotted the passenger window of the Town and Country van rolling down.

"Hey, pretty lady." Hoop giggled.

Alesia looked inside of the van and saw Hoop and Spanish Dan. She smiled as she walked to the passenger window.

"I see ole boy is free, what happened in there?" Hoop asked.

"He had a bench trial with the judge and the judge ruled in his favor. He also got accepted into college."

"College?" Hoop asked, not believing his ears.

"Yeah! Medical school in Georgia."

"I'm proud of the little nigga and glad that he finally is able to make it out of the hood." Hoop said. *"I have to murk this nigga ASAP. He isn't making it to Georgia."* He thought.

"Me too. I'm proud of him." Alesia said, "So are you back in the hood or what?"

"Nah! I'm in Florida. I just came to visit a few family members, but I'll stay in touch. You know my number." Hoop said, as he signaled Spanish Dan to pull off.

"I do. I have to get going, bye Hoop." Alesia said as she stepped away from the van. She walked to her car, opened the door and slid inside. She couldn't believe how lucky Bones was to escape with all the stuff he had endured throughout his life. *"I hope his lady knows that he has enough enemies to fill Fenway Park."* She thought as she put the car in drive and pulled off.

Spanish Dan drove off and pulled to a light. He looked over at Hoop and asked. "What we going to do with this little nigga Bones?"

"I don't know. I'm still contemplating whether I should continue to let him breathe. I know if I murder him my mother would be disappointed and probably disown me. She always stated if a person can make it out of the hood then he shall prevail out of the hood and by the little nigga going to college that's making it out of the hood. I must honestly say I'm proud of him. I did cause all this stuff to happen and I must take responsibility for my actions, but that damn shootout keeps nagging at me."

"You have all the money in the world and you worried about a damn shootout. His boy Menace was different; he was the puppet master in the P. We all know that Menace didn't like you for years and it probably was him who had egged Bones on to murk Speedy and to shoot at you. It's your call if you want to leave it alone or dust him off. It doesn't matter to me."

"I'm going to let him breathe and enjoy his life. He deserves it after his dream of playing ball was shattered." Hoop said as he made his mind up to let go of the hostility he had for Bones.

Chapter 55

Mrs. Mary sat in her office chair looking out the window of her office. Over the years her health was deteriorating. She showed early signs of dementia and became diabetic. She saw her grandson walking toward her office. She scooted the chair back and waited for him to knock on the door.

Bones reached his grandmother's office, hesitated and then knocked three times. The door opened as her secretary allowed him in. Mrs. Mary was sitting behind her desk in a comfortable chair with some papers in front of her. Bones sat in front of the desk, grabbed his grandmother's hand and kissed it.

"Grandma, I love you."

Mrs. Mary smiled and slid a piece of paper toward him. Bones picked up the paper and read it. He was shocked to see that B.H.A. (Boston Housing Authority) stripped T.M.C. from their control over the project. He lowered his head for a few minutes, raised it and displayed tears. He knew how hard his grandmother worked on keeping the residents in control of the project. He tried to speak but no words came out. He gathered his thoughts and looked at all the gray hair his grandmother accumulated over the past few months. He knew the gray stemmed from years of stress. Bones reached in his pocket and slid the acceptance letter across the desk. She picked it up, read it and slid it back.

"This project is not your home. Go and live your life down south. You have caused so much pain, heartache and destruction that you are lucky to make it out of the city alive."

Bones looked at his grandmother and knew that she was telling the truth. He thought about his father, mother and other family members.

"The only reason why I am here is to show you I changed and to see my family."

"If your family wants to see you then they will come anywhere you are. I congratulate you on your change of heart, but deep down are you really a changed person?"

"Yes! This is my last time in the project. I'm going to live my life with my lady." Bones said, as he rose from his chair. He leaned over and kissed his grandmother on her cheek, forehead and hand. He backed away and walked out of the office. He stood on the stairs, looked at the sky and walked to his mother's car.

* * * * * *

Alesia saw her son walking around the project aimlessly. She called him over and gave him a hug and a kiss. She looked him in his eyes and told him. "I know what you are about to do and I know we discussed the possibilities of retaliation, but leave it alone. He made his decision to leave the hood and please honor his decision."

"What do you mean leave the hood?"

"Alfred got accepted into college. He is going to live out his dreams."

"So, what that has to do with my father. Because of him I have no father. He shattered my dream of having my old man around and I'm about to look him in the eye and tell him who my dad was before I kill him." Tragdon said before he walked away.

What Alesia didn't know was that Hoop a week prior offered her son 20,000 cash to murder Bones. At first Tragdon declined the offer, but when Hoop told him if he didn't do it then he and his mother would be killed together. He became scared and instead of telling Bones about the hit that Hoop placed on him he decided to do it. He went home and stayed to himself and that's when his mother told him that Bones was the one responsible for the murder of his father. Hearing that Bones was responsible for killing Mr. Millionaire, Tragdon decided to get his revenge by killing Bones and collecting the 20,000 from Hoop.

Tragdon walked to Centre Street and saw a Town and Country van pull up. He stared at the tinted windows and kept walking. He heard someone shout his name and looked closer at the van. He saw Hoop's face staring at him. He walked over and started talking to Hoop through the window. Hoop told him to scratch the hit on Bones and passed him 5,000 dollars. Tragdon took the money but still decided once he caught Bones sleeping, he was going to kill him in the honor of his father. He gave dap to Hoop and walked away. As he walked through the project, he saw Bones walking to a car and called out his name.

Bones heard someone call his name and saw that it was Tragdon. He walked toward him with a smile on this face. *"This is one little nigga that I would love to see make it out of the hood and if I could help him I would."* Bones thought as he neared Tragdon.

Tragdon had his left hand in his jacket pocket clutching his gun. He planned to shoot Bones through his jacket and then when he fell pump a few more slugs into his upper body. As he was ready to pull the trigger flashbacks of all the good things Bones did for him came into his mind from the day Bones showed him to dribble the ball effectively, to giving him sound advice on staying out of the hood and how he always gave him money when he saw him. *"I don't know what my father did to him, but I can't kill him. He was for my best interest and I'm going to be for him."* He pulled his hand out of his pocket and reached and gave Bones a hug. "Congratulations my mother told me that you are on your way to college."

"Yes. I got accepted into medical school down south. I know I made a lot of mistakes and did some foolish things that I paid my debt for but none of it was worth me losing my leg and almost my life. Take heed and get away from this hood shit. We already lost Juicy, Speedy, Skitzo and Menace. Who is next?"

"None of us." Tragdon said, as he placed his hand in his pocket and pulled out the cash that Hoop gave him. "Here this is yours. This is all the money you gave me over the years." Tragdon lied.

"Thanks, little man. I never knew you were saving the money." Bones said perplexed at the generous donation of the youngster.

"Anything for those who I idolize and those who always treated me right. I want to tell you something, but I don't know how you would take it so I'm going to keep it to myself."

"What you mean?"

"Just forget about what I had just said and bring about a change so others like me can follow and be productive in life."

"I will dawg. I promise you I will." Bones said, as he gave Tragdon a hug. He felt the bulge of Tragdon's gun, released his grip and walked away. He wondered what Tragdon wanted to tell him, but if it wasn't meant for him to know then it wasn't. He made it to his mother's car and got in the passenger side.

The ride to Newton was in silence. The only sound in the car was Lynn sobbing. She wasn't sobbing for something he had done wrong. Her tears was that of joy. She was relieved that her son was leaving the streets and entering college.

Bones hated when his mother had cried. He always felt her tears were that of sorrow. He looked at her and said. "I'm sorry for killing your boyfriend back in the day and all the other stuff I had done to make you cry. I can honestly say I made you cry today with tears of joy instead of tears of sorrow."

"It's okay son. It's okay." Lynn said, as she thought about Mr. Millionaire and how much the young kid Tragdon, resemble him. "If you remembered how Mr. Millionaire looked then you would know that the young kid Tragdon is some type of kin to him or probably his son. He just resemble him too much. His mother fooled a lot of people in the project, but she didn't fool me. It took me sometime to realize who she was or what she was about. That's why I put her down with my crew, so I can monitor her actions."

"What?" Bones said, as he looked at his moms. Hearing this is when he realized that Tragdon wanted to tell him who Mr. Millionaire was to him or even possibly exact some type of revenge. *"Damn if the little nigga had that killer in him, he would of have been the only nigga who could have shattered my dream of being a doctor."*

Lynn pulled up to Bones house and parked in the driveway. "Listen to me son. You have a beautiful lady who loves you, cares for you and supports you. Make her your all and you will always be rewarded with the best that life has to offer." She said, as she leaned over and kissed him.

Bones said a few words to his mother and got out of the car. He walked to the front of the house and saw a newspaper outside the front door. He picked it up and read the caption. "AT THE AGE OF 12 SHYHEIM CARTER WAS THE 1ST JUVENILE CHARGED UNDER THE BARTON'S LAW FOR A VIOLENT CRIME. NOW 18 YRS OLD, UPON RELEASE THIS WEEK WILL HE CONTINUE THE PATTERN OF VIOLENCE THAT MOST JUVENILES CONTINUE TO DO ONCE RELEASED." He looked at the picture of Scar and even though Bones crew and Scar's crew were mortal enemies. He wished him the best on his transition. *"All the shit I went through to find my inner peace, I hope he can make that same transition and live out his dreams. I may never know because I have no plans to cross paths with him and if I do, I will apologize to him for the friction I created years back with him."* Bones said to himself as he used his key to open the door.

Coming 2021

3 Pounds

Of

<u>Pressure</u>

Pressure is Applied

Preview

3 Pounds of Pressure: Pressure
<u>Is Applied</u>

Shyheim "Scar" Carter

The sound of Scar's cousin Faury's woke him up. He sat up in his bed. *"These nightmares have to stop,"* Scar thought, as he picked up his phone and saw that a whole day has passed since he was released from juvenile detention. He got off the bed, walked downstairs and ate the breakfast his mother prepared before she went to work. After he ate, he took a shower, got dressed and then left. He walked to the commuter rail train station and sat on a bench. Fifteen minutes later his train pulled up, he stepped on and found a seat. As the train made its way to Ruggels Train Station he reflected on the conversation he had with his father before he was arrested and how he had lied about what really happened.

"I have to go to Arizona to see my dad ASAP." Scar said as he thought about what led him to spend the last five years in the Department of Youth Services.

The commute from Norwood to Academy homes was a little less than an hour. Scar had to use the commuter rail train system from Norwood to Ruggels MBTA station, and then board a city bus to Academy Homes. This was Norwood his first time returning to his housing projects since age eleven. The bus stopped and Scar stepped off. Scar was dressed in a charcoal gray linen short set and gray Top Ten Adidas. He looked at the buildings that made up Academy homes, swallowed his spit, walked across the street and into the project.

Scattered around the courtyard were groups of people playing dice, hustling and drinking beer. He walked toward a crowd of niggas his age.

"What's good," Scar greeted the group.

"Who you?" A youngster named Little Barry asked, stepping forward.

Scar held his guard and looked at all the unfamiliar faces. Scar was born and raised in Academy Homes, his family's name held weight around the city and he would be damned if he took shorts from anyone.

"Scar. I'm from out here," He replied, as he pointed to his old building on Weaver Way.

"Oh yeah, who's your peeps? Name some names?" Another youngster named Red asked as he lifted his shirt to reveal the handle of a Ruger P89.

Scar wasn't ready to reveal who his father was because he intended to carve his own rep in the project. He knew if he tried to be brave that he would be left where he was standing.

"My father is Stretch." Scar answered.

"Uncle Stretch?" Red asked, as he let his shirt drop over the gun

"Yeah! That's my dad," Scar said.

A stocky nigga wearing a throwback Dale Murphy Jersey stepped forward, "okay, I remember you now. You were all over the news when you were a little kid. You just now coming home from that shit."

"Yeah!" Scar said.

"He's official tissue. Let me introduce you to the team dawg," Pitt said, as he reached and gave Scar the three-finger salute. "This is Red, Little Barry, Homicide and I am Pitt. "So, they call you Scar huh?"

"Yeah! The name is Scar," Scar answered, as he turned his face to the side to show the pear-shape scar on his left cheek.

"Welcome home nigga. Where's your Atlanta Braves cap at?"

"I don't have one. Scar answered.

"What time is it? Pitt asked.

"It's a quarter past twelve," Little Barry informed.

"It's still early. Come on," Pitt said, as he led the way to the project Bodega. "Over the years a lot of niggas got killed fucking with us. You see that project across the street," he pointed to Bromley Heath Street.

"Yeah! Scar said.

"That's our number one rivals. Watch out for these two cousins named Bones and Castro they are two wild ass niggas. They are at the top of our murder list."

A black Range Rover pulled up to the curb. A light skin, chubby older head with long cornrows that reached the bottom of his neck stepped out with a throwback Hank Aaron Jersey.

"Who is that," Scar asked.

"Yo! That's Free. He's an older head from the Light Side." Pitt said.

"The Light Side where is that? Scar asked.

"There's two sides of the project the Light Side and the Dark Side. The Washington Street and Codman Park area is the Light Side and this area where we hang out is called the Dark Side." Pitt informed.

"Oh! Okay." Scar said, as Free made his way up the stairs and into the crowd. He stopped at Scar and saw that Scar had no Atlanta Braves hat on.

"Where are you from?" Free asked.

"The A," Scar replied.

"What's your name little nigga?" Free asked.

"Scar." Scar answered.

"That's Uncle Stretch's son," Little Barry said.

"Oh yeah! Where's your daddy at? He still hiding in Arizona," Free laughed.

Scar felt disrespected by the line of questioning and the manner how Free approached him. He looked at Pitt and back at Free.

"I see he got games. I'll be sure to tell my father what you said." Scar said.

"Tell him. No-one's scared of him. Since you talk tough and act

264

tough, to be around here you have to put in work, little nigga. Someone give this nigga a hammer. He's going across the street to handle his business. That's your initiation, little nigga," Free said, pointing to Bromley-Heath Street Project.

"Nah! That's not a good look. Don't you see all those police cruisers across the street," Pitt cut in.

Scar gave Free a devious smile. In time, he knew Free was going to be a problem that needed to be handled. He didn't know when, but he knew it would be soon.

Free stepped off and made his way back to his Range Rover. He sat in the driver's seat for a while staring at Scar. He still remembered the day when Uncle Stretch shot him three times and now that Scar was back in the project Free would use Scar to bring Uncle Stretch back to town. He put the Range Rover in drive, pulled off and headed down the street.

"You good? That's Free. He held the project down for years," Red said patting Scar on his shoulder.

"Let's go and get some more troops, head downtown and get him his Atlanta Braves hat," Pitt said.

They walked to the Four Squares, rounded up six more people and walked to Stony Brook Train Station. They hopped on the train. Everyone had on different types of Braves hats except Scar. He felt like an outcast. This was Scar's first time in the midst of some real gangsters. His adrenaline pumped as he was ready to prove himself. He eyed a few pretty girls as they boarded the train.

"Yo! You want to hold the heat?" Little Barry asked.

"Yeah!" Scar said calmly.

"Come on," Homicide said, as he walked to the back of the train.

When they reached the back of the train Little Barry reached in his waist, pulled out the bulky .9mm and passed it to Scar. An older lady watched the exchange, shook her head and turned away. She couldn't understand why the younger generation was so infatuated with killing one another. Scar walked back to where the rest of the crew was posted and took a seat. A couple of stops later the train stopped at Jackson Square.

Jackson Square was home to their rivals, Bromley Heath Street. They all stood on their seats looking to see if they saw any Miami Heat Hats. Five stops later, they stepped off the train and headed toward the store. They walked into a hat store and studied the Atlanta Braves' caps. Scar stared at a gray Braves cap that matched his linen short set.

"Pick one." Pitt said.

Scar pointed to the gray Atlanta Braves cap. Pitt bought the cap and watched as Scar tossed it on his head.

"I love it." Scar said looking in the mirror.

They walked out of the store. As they crossed the street, they saw a bunch of niggas flooding the street and sidewalk wearing Cleveland Cavaliers caps.

"Who's those niggas?" Scar asked.

"That's C.V.O. (Cape Verdean Outlaws). Their whole crew is Cape Verdeans. They be up on the Bowdoin and Hamilton area," Pitt said, as he threw up his fist to his man Sauce Money.

Pitt opened the door to Expressions Clothing Store and walked in. Scar saw over a dozen Cape Verdeans with Washington Nationals' Caps on. He knew from his travels in the juvenile system that Wendover Street wore the caps, and that they were having a bloody war with C.V.O.

"SCAR!" a Wendover Street Gang member named Rocky shouted.

Scar turned around and saw Rocky. He walked up to him and gave him a hug. They spoke briefly and then rejoined their circles.

"I see those Mission Hill niggas are deep," Pitt said, as he stared at the pack of Michigan Wolverine caps near the sneaker section. Scar reached in his waist for the Ruger. He was ready to squeeze and clear the store out. "Nah! Not here. We ain't at war with them," Pitt informed.

Scar listened to Pitt and walked toward the Adidas section. He picked up a pair of blue, red, and white Top Ten Adidas. "How much?" Scar asked.

"Eighty-five dollars," the sales lady said.

Scar paid for the sneakers, a T-shirt, and some jeans. They walked out of the store and hopped on the train back to the hood. They made it back to the project with no problems. As soon as they stepped in the courtyard, they saw Free in front of a building with a few older heads.

Free saw them and made his way toward the pack of youngsters. He stopped at Scar and reached for the bag. "What's in the bag?" Free asked. Scar pulled the bag back. Free flipped Scar's Atlanta Braves cap off of his head onto the ground. "You heard me, what's in the bag?"

Scar dropped the bag and reached for his waist. Free saw him clutching his waist and laughed. "I wish you would new jack. Remember that you're a new jack around here, remember that." Free said, "don't forget to tell your daddy to come out of hiding."

Little Barry grabbed Scar by the waist and pulled him back. Pitt stepped in the middle and pushed Free back. "Don't touch me little nigga," Free barked. "I will spank that little nigga in this courtyard and dump his body in that dumpster" Free said pointing to Scar and then the dumpster. "You wish," Scar responded, as he picked up his cap, brushed it off, and tossed it on his head. "You're a punk-like your daddy," Free said, as he walked away from the crowd.

"*This nigga got me fucked up, I'm going to have to kill him quickly and, in a hurry,*" Scar thought, as he saw a Mercedes-Benz S-class pull up into the parking lot. He watched as a slim built, brown skin nigga step out with an Atlanta Braves cap.

"Yo! Pitt. Who's that?" Scar asked.

"That's the nigga Riot. He's part of our circle. He was raised in St. Joe's, but he reps the A."

"Oh! I was in juvey with a few niggas from St. Joes." Scar said.

"He's a good nigga. He's touching some decent paper out here too." Pitt said.

"I can see," Scar said, as he stared at Riot's chain.

Riot walked over and gave dap to Pitt and when he reached Scar, he introduced himself and stuck out three fingers. Scar gave him the three-finger handshake.

"I like that A hat," Scar said.

"I try to get all the flavor that niggas can't find." Riot said, "What are you new to the hood?"

"Yeah and No! I'm originally from out here, but I had been in juvie for a while."

"That's what's up. When you come home?" Riot asked.

"The other day."

"Okay." Riot said, as he reached in his pocket and pulled out a knot of money, peeled off a few bills and passed it to Scar.

"Good look," Scar said, as he took the money and put it in his pocket.

"There's no need to thank me. Real niggas do real things. We going to get up. Let me make these runs," Riot said as he gave dap and walked away.

Scar thoughts reverted to how disrespectful Free was. *"Don't this nigga know that it only takes three pounds of pressure to pull a trigger."* Scar thought, as flashbacks came to him the day Broad Day Jay showed him how to hold a gun.

Made in the USA
Middletown, DE
24 November 2021

52697348R00156